ANDREW AND MURIEL'S
HEALTHY HAPPY HOLIDAYS COOKBOOK
"Our Perfect Recipes for Healthier Holidays"

MURIEL ANGOT

WITH ANDREW LESSMAN

PHOTOGRAPHY: LINDSEY ELTINGE
COVER PHOTOGRAPHY: JEFF STROHECKER
STYLIST: LOETTA EARNEST
SOUS CHEF: JESUSITA MONTES
ASSISTANT: KYLE KLEIN
ART DIRECTION: EDWARD MOSS

Published by the Andrew Lessman Foundation
430 Parkson Road, Henderson, NV 89011

Printed in the United States of America.

First Printing, October 2013

ISBN 978-0-578-12954-9

*To the family, friends and food we love
and enjoy each holiday season.*

Andrew's sister Gail, Andrew and Muriel cooking together.

ABOUT THE AUTHOR

 **Muriel Angot** was born and raised in the world's center of fine cuisine – Paris, France; however, it would take Muriel a couple of decades to rediscover her Parisian culinary roots, since she initially followed in her parents' footsteps studying Fine Art at the Sorbonne University in Paris. After college, Muriel's innate curiosity and desire to explore the world saw her leave France, spending time in Australia, Fiji, New Zealand and South America, until she fell in love with the United States where she established a beauty and wellness business in Aspen, Colorado. It wasn't until Muriel chose to attend cooking school that her true passion captured her and since that time, has never let go.

Like many French families, all the members of Muriel's family take pride in their abilities in the kitchen. But it was Muriel's paternal grandmother, Simone, who was to have the greatest influence, since she was the chef and owner of a restaurant in Picardie, France – a small city in the countryside just outside Paris. Some of Muriel's fondest childhood memories are of helping her grandmother create all the classic French dishes that were served at her restaurant. The special moments she shared with her grandmother in the culturally rich environment of an authentic French kitchen were to shape the rest of Muriel's life.

When Muriel moved from Colorado to California, the move presented an opportunity for a career change and with great trepidation she decided to take the plunge. Despite hearing how challenging and difficult it would be, Muriel followed her dream and attended Le Cordon Bleu cooking school in Paris – the same school attended by Julia Child. Ultimately, she graduated #1 in her class and now considers herself blessed to combine her two greatest passions – cooking and wellness.

FOREWORD
from Andrew and Muriel

 When I think about the Holidays and their challenges to healthy eating, I am reminded of the opening lines of the novel "*A Tale of Two Cities*" by Charles Dickens. Of course, this classic novel was not about healthy eating around the holidays, but because his words depict a world of contrasts and extremes, they aptly describe the challenges we face each holiday season. Just for fun and because they are among the most eloquent words ever written in the English language, I have included them below:

> *It was the best of times, it was the worst of times, it was the age of wisdom, it was the age of foolishness, it was the epoch of belief, it was the epoch of incredulity, it was the season of Light, it was the season of Darkness, it was the spring of hope, it was the winter of despair, we had everything before us, we had nothing before us, we were all going direct to Heaven, we were all going direct the other way…*

My apologies to Mr. Dickens for borrowing his beautiful words to describe the extremes we face each holiday season; but, his words apply so well to the holidays since they truly are the very "best of times." However, when it comes to what we eat, they can also be the very "worst of times." For Muriel and me, the challenges start around Halloween and continue through the seemingly endless "food-centered" Thanksgiving and Christmas gatherings, events and parties. It isn't until sometime after the New Year that we can all take stock of the holiday fallout and, once again, somehow manage to find the inspiration necessary to undertake our New Year's Resolutions.

Muriel and I hope that this book's recipes provide an easy, delicious and healthier way to enjoy the Holidays. Of course, we recognize that the holidays are meant to be enjoyed, so this book's recipes are not about bland deprivation, but are all about making holiday eating healthier and with fewer calories without sacrificing enjoyment. Our ultimate goal is that we all reach January even healthier than we were before the holidays. This book contains the tools that Muriel and I use to achieve that every year.

Since we started this Foreword with Charles Dickens' opening lines to "A Tale of Two Cities," it is only fair that we finish with his inspiring closing words:

> *It is a far, far better thing that I do, than I have ever done; it is a far, far better rest that I go to than I have ever known.*

My sincere apologies if we got a bit too literary here, but we are both so often amazed at the power and wisdom of words written so long ago.

Happy Healthy Holidays – and Every Day! Bon appétit!

Andrew and Muriel

Because you've asked...
some additional pictures of Lincoln.

CONTENTS

Appetizers

Soups and Salads

Soups and Salads (continued)

11
QUINOA SALAD WITH
BEETS, CLEMENTINE AND
POMEGRANATE

12
SWEET POTATO, APPLE AND
KALE SALAD WITH
YELLOW RAISINS

Main Courses

13
MURIEL AND ANDREW'S
TURKEY WITH SPICE RUB

16
MIRIAM'S
TURKEY TACOS

14
TURKEY CABBAGE CUPS
WITH ASIAN DIPPING SAUCE

17
WHOLE SALMON FILLET WITH
CILANTRO AND
PISTACHIO PESTO

15
SUZETTE'S
TURKEY LOAF

18
MURIEL'S KALE, RICOTTA
AND PUMPKIN LASAGNA

Sauces

19
HERB AND SPICE
GRAVY

20
FRESH CRANBERRY SAUCE
WITH DRIED FIGS AND MINT

Stuffing

Side Dishes

Desserts

 33
PUMPKIN "PIE" PARFAITS

 35
BLACK & WHITE CAKE

 34
BLUEBERRY AND PECAN
CRUMBLE

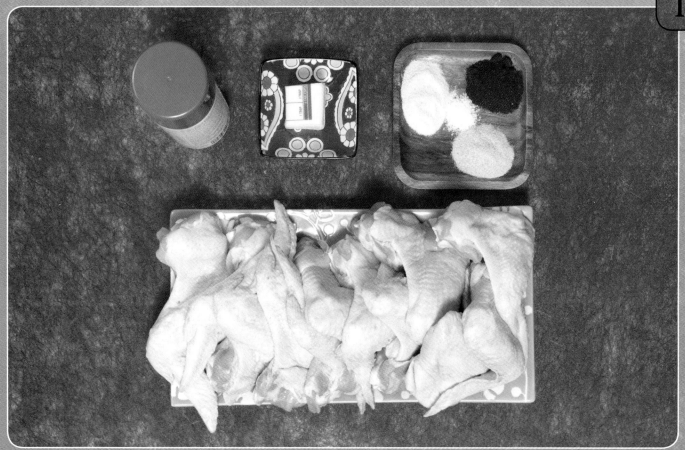

ANDREW'S MOM'S "MUSHY" CHICKEN WINGS

20 WINGS • PREPARATION: 5 MINUTES • COOKING: 18–20 MINUTES • EASY

Andrew's mom made these when he was a child and they are still his favorite today. He even enjoyed them throughout college, because they were so simple and easy for him to make and always delicious. Andrew exclusively used butter in the past, but nowadays he blends butter and olive oil to supply the moisture necessary for the powdered spices to stick to the wings. We all love these wings, but Andrew usually eats them all before anyone can get near them. He and his sister called them "mushy" as children, since they loved all the delicious "mushy" spices left at the bottom of the pan.

20 chicken wings

2 tbsp. butter, melted
(or olive oil)

Olive oil spray

1 tbsp. paprika

1 tbsp. garlic powder

1 tbsp. onion powder
(optional)

Kosher salt to taste

1 Preheat the broiler. Melt the butter in the microwave. Cover a baking sheet with foil lightly sprayed with olive oil and arrange chicken wings on the sheet.

2 Thoroughly coat chicken with melted butter or olive oil and lightly sprinkle with salt, garlic powder, onion powder (optional) and paprika.

3 Place wings under a preheated broiler for approximately 7 to 8 minutes. Skin should be nicely browned.

4 Remove pan from the oven, turn wings and once again, sprinkle other side salt, garlic powder, onion powder (optional) and paprika. Broil additional 5 minutes.

5 Remove from oven and turn wings over again. Sprinkle with the remaining spices and return to broiler a third time for 3-5 minutes, making sure the top side is nice and crisp.

6 Broil a few minutes more until desired crispness is achieved. Serve warm.

Nutrition Information

Serving Size **2 Wings**   Servings **10**

Calories	155	Potassium	153 mg
Calories from fat	77	Total Carbohydrates	1 g
Total Fat	9 g	Dietary Fiber	0 g
Cholesterol	6 mg	Sugars	0 g
Sodium	77 mg	Protein	19 g

Vitamin A	10 %	Folic Acid	1 %
Calcium	1 %	Vitamin B12	3 %
Iron	6 %	Pantothenic Acid	6 %
Vitamin D	1 %	Phosphorus	11 %
Vitamin E	3 %	Magnesium	4 %
Vitamin K	2 %	Zinc	9 %
Vitamin B1	2 %	Selenium	22 %
Vitamin B2	6 %	Copper	2 %
Niacin	23 %	Manganese	2 %
Vitamin B6	16 %		

OTHER BENEFICIAL NUTRIENTS (PER SERVING)

Omega-3 (ALA+EPA+DPA+DHA)	**196 mg**
Choline	44 mg
Beta-Carotene	182 mcg
Alpha-Carotene	4 mcg
Lutein & Zeaxanthin	129 mcg

MINI FRITTATA
WITH YAM AND PANCETTA

24 MINI FRITTATAS • PREPARATION: 20 MINUTES • COOKING: 18-20 MINUTES • EASY

This mini-Frittata (crustless quiche) is a delicious treat. You can include almost anything from mushrooms to vegetables like leeks, onions, spinach and more. Feel free to be creative! I find yams to be an excellent addition because they help bind things together so beautifully. You can also make a delicious vegetarian frittata by simply replacing the pancetta with another vegetable or tofu. It is just perfect for brunch or as a light appetizer before dinner.

Cooking spray

1 large yam

1 shallot, chopped

1 tsp. olive oil

3 eggs, beaten

1 cup egg white, beaten

¾ cup Swiss cheese, grated

1 oz. fresh thyme

4 oz. pancetta, diced

Salt and freshly ground
pepper to taste

A pinch of cayenne pepper
(optional)

1 Preheat oven to 375°. Peel, cube and steam the yam in a steamer basket for 10 to 15 minutes until soft.

2 Mash the yam and allow to cool.

3 Sauté the shallot in olive oil in a small skillet for 5 minutes until golden.

4 In a large bowl whisk together the eggs, egg whites, Swiss cheese, half of the thyme, sautéed shallots, mashed yam, pancetta, salt and pepper.

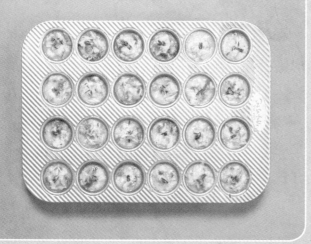

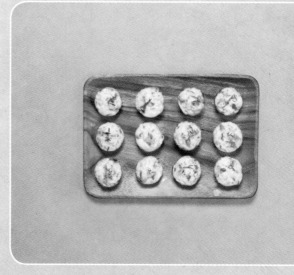

5 Lightly grease mini muffin pans with cooking spray. Spoon 1 to 2 tbsp. into each muffin cup. Bake for approximately 18 to 20 minutes.

6 Serve garnished with thyme and a tiny pinch of cayenne pepper.

Nutrition Information

Serving Size **1 Mini Frittata** Servings **24**

Calories	73	Potassium	79 mg
Calories from fat	50	Total Carbohydrates	3 g
Total Fat	6 g	Dietary Fiber	0 g
Cholesterol	28 mg	Sugars	1 g
Sodium	65 mg	Protein	3 g

Vitamin A	33 %	Vitamin B6	2 %
Vitamin C	1 %	Folic Acid	2 %
Calcium	2 %	Vitamin B12	2 %
Iron	1 %	Pantothenic Acid	2 %
Vitamin D	1 %	Phosphorus	4 %
Vitamin E	1 %	Magnesium	1 %
Vitamin K	1 %	Zinc	1 %
Vitamin B1	1 %	Selenium	6 %
Vitamin B2	5 %	Copper	1 %
Niacin	1 %	Manganese	2 %

OTHER BENEFICIAL NUTRIENTS (PER SERVING)

Omega-3 (ALA+EPA+DPA+DHA)	8 mg
Choline	20 mg
Beta-Carotene	971 mcg
Alpha-Carotene	1 mcg
Lutein & Zeaxanthin	32 mcg

Zucchini and Sweet Potato Latkes

12 - 15 LATKES • PREPARATION: 40 MINUTES • COOKING: 30 MINUTES • DIFFICULT

I love potato latkes, but since Andrew and I tend to avoid regular potatoes, sweet potatoes (or yams) or even zucchini make this a more nutritious, healthier alternative. It is a fairly time-consuming recipe, but truly worth the extra effort. It is especially delicious if you serve it with our Salmon Mousse (Recipe #4) or applesauce. Don't forget to squeeze the moisture from the zucchini and sweet potato beforehand. It is essential to the finished recipe. You can also add a pinch of cayenne pepper for a bit of extra spice.

1 zucchini (2 cups)

1 sweet potato (about 3 cups)

⅔ cup onion, grated

1 garlic clove, minced

2 eggs

1 tsp. baking powder

¾ cup flour (preferably Garbanzo)

Salt and freshly ground
    pepper to taste

Pinch of cayenne pepper
    (optional)

½ tsp. cumin

Olive oil spray

1 Preheat oven to 350°. Peel and grate the zucchini and sweet potato. Place in a paper towel and gently squeeze out as much moisture as possible.

2 In a bowl, combine the zucchini, sweet potato, onion, garlic, eggs, baking powder, flour, salt, pepper and cumin.

3 Form the mixture into small, round pancake/latkes. I make about 12 to 15.

4 Spray a large non-stick skillet with olive oil and cook the latkes over medium heat for 5 to 7 minutes on each side until they are a rich, golden hue.

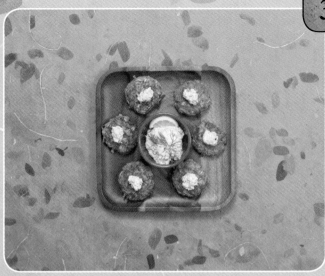

5 Transfer the browned latkes to a foil-lined baking sheet. Bake for 20 minutes in order to cook through.

6 Serve with applesauce or our Salmon Mousse (Recipe #4).

Nutrition Information

Serving Size **1 Latke**   Servings **15**

Calories	79	Potassium	304 mg
Calories from fat	16	Total Carbohydrates	13 g
Total Fat	2 g	Dietary Fiber	2 g
Cholesterol	25 mg	Sugars	1 g
Sodium	14 mg	Protein	2 g

Vitamin A	2 %	Vitamin B6	6 %
Vitamin C	12 %	Folic Acid	4 %
Calcium	2 %	Vitamin B12	1 %
Iron	3 %	Pantothenic Acid	3 %
Vitamin D	1 %	Phosphorus	8 %
Vitamin E	1 %	Magnesium	5 %
Vitamin K	2 %	Zinc	2 %
Vitamin B1	5 %	Selenium	9 %
Vitamin B2	4 %	Copper	4 %
Niacin	3 %	Manganese	20 %

OTHER BENEFICIAL NUTRIENTS (PER SERVING)

Omega-3 (ALA+EPA+DPA+DHA)	**17 mg**
Choline	**28 mg**
Beta-Carotene	**40 mcg**
Lutein & Zeaxanthin	**399 mcg**

SALMON MOUSSE

2 CUPS • PREPARATION: 15 MINUTES • COOKING: 0 MINUTES • VERY EASY

This is a lovely light appetizer. We first discovered it at a local seafood restaurant where we enjoyed their less healthy and much higher calorie version. We often eat it with gluten-free crackers, but love it as a vegetable dip with cucumbers, zucchini or on endive leaves. It also goes perfectly with our zucchini and sweet potato latkes (Recipe #3)!

½ cup fat-free yogurt

½ cup whipped or light cream cheese

1 oz. fresh dill, finely minced

½ tsp. horseradish (optional)

Juice of ½ lemon (approx. 1 tbsp.)

Freshly ground pepper to taste

Zest of ½ a lemon, grated

8 oz. smoked salmon, finely diced

A pinch of cayenne pepper

1 Mix the yogurt, cream cheese, dill, horseradish, lemon juice, crushed pepper and half of the lemon zest. You may also use a blender for this recipe.

2 Once mixed, add the chopped salmon and mix or blend for a few more seconds.

3 Garnish with remaining lemon zest and dill. (Sprinkle a pinch of cayenne pepper on top for a spicier treat.) Serve on cucumber slices, endive leaves or our Zucchini and Sweat Potato Latkes (Recipe #3).

Nutrition Information

Serving Size 2 Tablespoons   Servings **16**

Calories **32**	Potassium . . . . **82 mg**
Calories from fat **8**	Total Carbohydrates . . . . **1 g**
Total Fat . . . . **1 g**	Dietary Fiber . . . . **0 g**
Cholesterol . . . . . . **5 mg**	Sugars . . . . **1 g**
Sodium . . . . **181 mg**	Protein . . . . **4 g**

Vitamin A . . . . **3 %**	Folic Acid . . . . **2 %**
Vitamin C . . . . **3 %**	Vitamin B12 . . . . . . **10 %**
Calcium . . . . **5 %**	Pantothenic Acid . . . . **3 %**
Iron . . . . **1 %**	Phosphorus . . . . **8 %**
Vitamin D . . . . . . **24 %**	Magnesium . . . . **2 %**
Vitamin E . . . . **1 %**	Zinc . . . . **2 %**
Vitamin B1 . . . . **1 %**	Selenium . . . . **8 %**
Vitamin B2 . . . . **4 %**	Copper . . . . **2 %**
Niacin . . . . **4 %**	Manganese . . . . **1 %**
Vitamin B6 . . . . **2 %**	

OTHER BENEFICIAL NUTRIENTS (PER SERVING)

Omega-3 (ALA+EPA+DPA+DHA) . . **74 mg**
Choline . . . . 13 mg
Beta-Carotene . . . . 1 mcg

ARTICHOKE AND WHITE BEAN DIP

2 CUPS • PREPARATION: 10 MINUTES • COOKING: 0 MINUTES • VERY EASY

There are all sorts of yummy dips out there, but most of them contain enormous amounts of calories because of ingredients like mayonnaise. Here is my healthy, delicious alternative that we use at home with both steamed and fresh vegetables. It's a quick, easy and versatile recipe that is perfect anytime. You might need to keep an eye on it, since although it is meant as a dip, Andrew often eats it by the spoonful.

2 tbsp. olive oil

1 15 oz. can cannellini beans,
  drained and rinsed

1 small jar (7.5 oz.) artichoke
  hearts, drained and rinsed

⅓ cup Parmesan cheese

1 tbsp. lemon juice

A few sprigs of fresh thyme

Cayenne pepper to taste

Salt and freshly ground
  pepper to taste

1 Put all ingredients in a blender: olive oil, beans, artichoke hearts, Parmesan cheese, lemon juice, thyme and cayenne pepper. Blend for approximately 3 minutes until smooth. Salt and pepper to taste.

2 Garnish with a pinch of cayenne and a fresh sprig of thyme. Serve with cut celery, carrots, cherry tomatoes, steamed green beans or other cut vegetables.

Nutrition Information

Serving Size **2 Tablespoons**   Servings **16**

Calories **107**	Potassium . . . . . . **362 mg**
Calories from fat **23**	Total Carbohydrates . . . **15 g**
Total Fat . . . . **3 g**	Dietary Fiber . . . . **4 g**
Cholesterol . . . . **1 mg**	Sugars . . . . **1 g**
Sodium . . . . **34 mg**	Protein . . . . **6 g**

Vitamin C . . . . **2 %**	Pantothenic Acid . . . . **2 %**
Calcium . . . . **5 %**	Phosphorus . . . . **10 %**
Iron . . . . **7 %**	Magnesium . . . . **11 %**
Vitamin E . . . . **2 %**	Zinc . . . . **6 %**
Vitamin K . . . . **1 %**	Selenium . . . . **2 %**
Vitamin B1 . . . . . . **14 %**	Copper . . . . **10 %**
Vitamin B2 . . . . **3 %**	Manganese . . . . **13 %**
Niacin . . . . **3 %**	
Vitamin B6 . . . . **4 %**	
Folic Acid . . . . **27 %**	

OTHER BENEFICIAL NUTRIENTS (PER SERVING)

Choline . . . . **15 mg**
Beta–Carotene . . . . **2 mcg**
Lutein & Zeaxanthin . . . . **37 mcg**

APRICOT-SOY GLAZED DRUMETTES

20 DRUMETTES • PREPARATION: 10 MINUTES • COOKING: 15-18 MINUTES • EASY

We love the sweet and savory blend of flavors of these drumettes. They are perfect for the holidays, but they are a real crowd-pleaser year-round. They are quick and easy to make and although I find them a little messy to eat — Andrew says he loves their delicious gooeyness. For a change of pace, we sometimes use orange marmalade instead of apricot preserve. Larger drumettes can be precooked in the oven at 425° and then you turn them over and switch to broil until the drumettes reach their desired combination of gooeyness and crispiness.

20 chicken drumettes

1 cup apricot preserve

1 cup low-sodium soy sauce

1 tsp. garlic powder

1 tsp. onion powder

1 tsp. red chili flakes (optional)

1 tbsp. ginger, grated

1 Preheat broiler. In a medium bowl, prepare marinade by mixing together the apricot preserve, soy sauce, garlic and onion powders, chili flakes and ginger.

2 Place the chicken and marinade in a large ziplock bag turning the closed bag to coat each drumette. (This can be reserved in the refrigerator for ½ to 1 hour, if you like.)

3 Arrange the marinated drumettes on a baking sheet covered with tin foil and spoon additional marinade over them until thoroughly coated.

4 Place under a preheated broiler for 7 minutes. Turn and broil for an additional 7 minutes until cooked through and golden in color.

5 Arrange on a platter and serve with remaining sauce from baking pan.

Nutrition Information

Serving Size **2 Drumettes**　　　　　　　　Servings **10**

Calories	93	Potassium	88 mg
Calories from fat	30	Total Carbohydrates	6 g
Total Fat	3 g	Dietary Fiber	0 g
Cholesterol	0 mg	Sugars	4 g
Sodium	244 mg	Protein	10 g

Vitamin A	2 %	Folic Acid	1 %
Vitamin C	1 %	Vitamin B12	2 %
Calcium	1 %	Pantothenic Acid	3 %
Iron	3 %	Phosphorus	6 %
Vitamin D	1 %	Magnesium	2 %
Vitamin E	1 %	Zinc	4 %
Vitamin B1	1 %	Selenium	11 %
Vitamin B2	3 %	Copper	2 %
Niacin	12 %	Manganese	2 %
Vitamin B6	8 %		

OTHER BENEFICIAL NUTRIENTS (PER SERVING)

Omega-3 (ALA+EPA+DPA+DHA)	88 mg
Choline	24 mg
Beta-Carotene	29 mcg
Lutein & Zeaxanthin	13 mcg

PUMPKIN SOUP
with TURMERIC and RED LENTILS

8 CUPS • PREPARATION: 20 MINUTES • COOKING: 35 MINUTES • MEDIUM

After making our Favorite Soups Cookbook, it is always fun to return to making soups again and this soup is just delicious. Pumpkin is a holiday favorite and we love the rich texture that it gives this flavorful soup. It is perfect for fall and winter. Andrew always reminds me that pumpkin is a great source of lycopene, while turmeric and curry are among the very healthiest of spices. As you may have noticed from our other recipes, we try to use these and other healthy spices as often as possible.

1 tbsp. coconut oil	4 cups broth (preferably turkey)	1 tsp. curry powder
1 red onion, chopped	1 cup red lentils	1 tsp. cinnamon
2 cloves garlic, minced	1 13.5 oz. can light coconut milk	Salt and freshly ground
2 red apples (1½ cups), cubed	1 tbsp. agave	pepper to taste
1 15 oz. can pure pumpkin (not pie mix)	1 tsp. turmeric	¼ cup scallions, minced

1 In a large pot over medium heat, melt the coconut oil and sauté the onion, garlic and apples for 5 minutes until the onion becomes translucent.

2 Add the pumpkin, broth, lentils, coconut milk, agave, turmeric, curry, cinnamon, salt and pepper. Cook for about 25 to 30 minutes until the lentils are soft and tender.

3 Pour into a blender and mix for 2 to 3 minutes until soup is smooth.

4 Garnish with a few scallions and serve warm

Nutrition Information

Serving Size **1 Cup**		Servings **8**

Calories **191**	Potassium . . . . . . **629 mg**	
Calories from fat . . . **118**	Total Carbohydrates . . . **14 g**	
Total Fat . . . . **13 g**	Dietary Fiber . . . . **2 g**	
Cholesterol . . . . **0 mg**	Sugars . . . . **8 g**	
Sodium . . . . **290 mg**	Protein . . . . **4 g**	

Vitamin A . . . . . . **191 %**	Folic Acid. . . . . **10 %**
Vitamin C . . . . **12 %**	Vitamin B12. . . . . . . **1 %**
Calcium . . . . **6 %**	Pantothenic Acid . . . . **4 %**
Iron . . . . **19 %**	Phosphorus. . . . . . . **11 %**
Vitamin E. . . . . **4 %**	Magnesium. . . . . . . **11 %**
Vitamin K . . . . **43 %**	Zinc . . . . **4 %**
Vitamin B1 . . . . **4 %**	Selenium . . . . **1 %**
Vitamin B2. . . . . **5 %**	Copper. . . . . **12 %**
Niacin . . . . **8 %**	Manganese . . . . **36 %**
Vitamin B6. . . . . **6 %**	

OTHER BENEFICIAL NUTRIENTS (PER SERVING)

Choline. . . . . **18 mg**
Beta-Carotene. . . . . **4,393 mcg**
Alpha-Carotene . . . . **2,687 mcg**
Lutein & Zeaxanthin. . . . . **337 mcg**

BUTTERNUT SQUASH SOUP
WITH APPLE AND CURRY

6 - 8 CUPS • PREPARATION: 20 MINUTES • COOKING: 70 MINUTES • MEDIUM

I felt I had to include this entry from our Favorite Soups Cookbook, since so many folks had told me they used it around the holidays. It is rich and satisfying while also using three of Andrew's favorite protective spices: cinnamon, nutmeg and curry. It is an excellent source of protein, fiber and protective phytonutrients. We got the idea for our version of this soup from our friend Carrie who is the mother of Andrew's goddaughter Devyn.

1 butternut squash, cut in half – approximately 1½ to 2 lbs.

1 tbsp. coconut oil

1 medium red onion (10 oz.)

2 cloves of garlic

1 medium apple (6 oz.), peeled and sliced

4 cups chicken broth

1 tbsp. of curry powder

1 tsp. cinnamon

1 tsp. ground nutmeg

Pinch of salt and pepper

¼ cup pecan halves, sautéed

1 Preheat oven to 400°. Sprinkle each half of the squash with half of the cinnamon and half of the nutmeg. Roast for 45 minutes. Let cool and scoop out the flesh.

2 In a 4- to 6-quart stock pot over medium heat, melt the coconut oil and sauté the onion, garlic and apple for 5 minutes.

3 Add broth, curry powder, the remaining cinnamon and nutmeg, and squash, and bring to a boil. Reduce heat to low and simmer for 20 minutes. Add salt and pepper to taste.

4 Purée in a blender or food processor working in small batches until smooth.

5 Serve in individual bowls with sautéed pecans sprinkled on top.

Nutrition Information

Serving Size **1 Cup**   Servings **8**

Calories	**115**	Potassium	**600 mg**
Calories from fat	**40**	Total Carbohydrates	**15 g**
Total Fat	**5 g**	Dietary Fiber	**5 g**
Cholesterol	**3 mg**	Sugars	**3 g**
Sodium	**50 mg**	Protein	**3 g**

Vitamin A	**150 %**	Folic Acid	**8 %**
Vitamin C	**30 %**	Vitamin B12	**9 %**
Calcium	**8 %**	Pantothenic Acid	**6 %**
Iron	**9 %**	Phosphorus	**14 %**
Vitamin E	**2 %**	Magnesium	**12 %**
Vitamin K	**3 %**	Zinc	**5 %**
Vitamin B1	**9 %**	Selenium	**6 %**
Vitamin B2	**6 %**	Copper	**14 %**
Niacin	**21 %**	Manganese	**36 %**
Vitamin B6	**11 %**		

OTHER BENEFICIAL NUTRIENTS (PER SERVING)

Omega-3 (ALA)	**30 mg**
Beta-Carotene	**3,600 mcg**
Alpha-Carotene	**700 mcg**
Gamma Tocopherol	**2 mg**

SWEET POTATO SPICE SOUP

10 – 12 CUPS • PREPARATION: 30 MINUTES • COOKING: 25 MINUTES • DIFFICULT

Since sweet potatoes are a staple around the holidays, we had to bring back this delicious soup from our Favorite Soups Cookbook. I love and enjoy sweet potatoes today, but they were not available when I was growing up in France. I first heard of them when I was 12 years old while reading Margaret Mitchell's book "Gone with the Wind," but I had to wait more than a decade to try them here in America. Now, I love them and this soup is perfect for the holidays!

3 tbsp. coconut oil

2 medium brown onions,
    1 chopped; 1 minced and
    reserved for garnish

2 cloves garlic, peeled and
    minced

1 tsp. Garam Masala Indian
    spice mix

½ tsp. turmeric

1 tsp. cumin

1 tsp. coriander

4¼ cups chicken broth

2 cups water

4 sweet potatoes, peeled and
    cubed

Salt and pepper to taste

⅓ cup coconut milk

Cinnamon Cream Garnish
(optional)

1 cup heavy whipping cream

1 tsp. cinnamon

1 In a large pot over medium heat, warm half the coconut oil and sauté one of the onions and the garlic until the onion is translucent.

2 Add the Garam Masala, turmeric, cumin and coriander stirring constantly for 3 minutes until aromatic.

3 Add the chicken broth, water and sweet potatoes, and bring to a boil. Reduce heat and simmer for 15 minutes until sweet potatoes are tender. After simmering, add the coconut milk. Add salt and pepper to taste.

4 In a separate small pan over medium heat, warm the remaining coconut oil and sauté the remaining onion for 7 minutes until golden and crisp. Set aside for later.

5 Purée the soup in a food processor or blender, working in small batches if needed and blending until smooth.

6 In a medium bowl, whisk the whipping cream with the cinnamon for 5 minutes. Serve in individual bowls garnished with cinnamon cream and minced onion. (Optional)

Nutrition Information

Serving Size **1 Cup**   Servings **12**

Calories	**86**	Potassium	**250 mg**
Calories from fat	**35**	Total Carbohydrates	**11 g**
Total Fat	**4 g**	Dietary Fiber	**2 g**
Cholesterol	**0 mg**	Sugars	**3 g**
Sodium	**151 mg**	Protein	**2 g**

Vitamin A	**123 %**	Folic Acid	**2 %**
Vitamin C	**14 %**	Vitamin B12	**1 %**
Calcium	**3 %**	Pantothenic Acid	**4 %**
Iron	**4 %**	Phosphorus	**4 %**
Vitamin E	**1 %**	Magnesium	**4 %**
Vitamin K	**1 %**	Zinc	**2 %**
Vitamin B1	**3 %**	Selenium	**1 %**
Vitamin B2	**2 %**	Copper	**5 %**
Niacin	**3 %**	Manganese	**11 %**
Vitamin B6	**6 %**		

OTHER BENEFICIAL NUTRIENTS (PER SERVING)

Omega-3 (ALA)	**2.8 mg**
Choline	**7 mg**
Beta-Carotene	**3,680 mcg**

Muriel's "Kaesar" Salad with Cranberries

10 CUPS • PREPARATION: 15 MINUTES • COOKING: 10 MINUTES • EASY

We are big fans of nutrient-rich kale at our house and I came up with this delicious salad while trying to create a healthier version of the famous Caesar salad. I call it my "Kaesar" salad and we love to top it with leftover turkey. I also add dried cranberries and pine nuts for a more festive look. It is rapidly becoming a favorite of everyone who tries it.

SALAD:

4 egg whites (reserve 1 yolk for dressing), about ½ cup

6 cups packed kale, chopped

1 cup dried cranberries

1 cup toasted pine nuts (optional)

1 oz. fresh mint leaves (reserve a few for dressing)

1 cup Parmesan cheese, shredded

DRESSING:

1 clove garlic, minced

1 egg yolk

1 tbsp. Dijon mustard

1 anchovy fillet

¼ cup lemon juice

½ cup Parmesan cheese, shredded

⅓ to ½ cup olive oil

½ tsp. red chili flakes

Salt and freshly ground pepper to taste

Zest of 1 lemon

1 Cook the egg whites in a small pan for 8 to 10 minutes. Chop finely.

2 In a large bowl combine the cooked egg whites, kale, cranberries, pine nuts, half of the mint, and a cup of the Parmesan cheese.

3 Make the dressing in a medium bowl or mini blender by combining the garlic, egg yolk, mustard, anchovy, lemon juice, remaining cheese and a few mint leaves. Slowly add olive oil blending until it begins to thicken. Blend in the chili flakes, salt and pepper.

4 Toss the salad with the dressing and garnish with lemon zest. Serve chilled.

Nutrition Information

Serving Size **1 Cup**   Servings **10**

Calories	**282**	Potassium	**256 mg**
Calories from fat	**189**	Total Carbohydrates	**15 g**
Total Fat	**21 g**	Dietary Fiber	**1 g**
Cholesterol	**28 mg**	Sugars	**8 g**
Sodium	**269 mg**	Protein	**9 g**

Vitamin A	**83 %**	Vitamin B6	**7 %**
Vitamin C	**87 %**	Folic Acid	**4 %**
Calcium	**22 %**	Vitamin B12	**4 %**
Iron	**5 %**	Pantothenic Acid	**2 %**
Vitamin D	**1 %**	Phosphorus	**14 %**
Vitamin E	**13 %**	Magnesium	**7 %**
Vitamin K	**368 %**	Zinc	**5 %**
Vitamin B1	**4 %**	Selenium	**11 %**
Vitamin B2	**11 %**	Copper	**31 %**
Niacin	**3 %**	Manganese	**16 %**

OTHER BENEFICIAL NUTRIENTS (PER SERVING)

Omega-3 (ALA+EPA+DPA+DHA)	**17 mg**
Choline	**18 mg**
Beta-Carotene	**2,399 mcg**
Alpha-Carotene	**23 mcg**
Lutein & Zeaxanthin	**3,338 mcg**

QUINOA SALAD WITH BEETS, CLEMENTINE AND POMEGRANATE

10 CUPS • PREPARATION: 30 MINUTES • COOKING: 30 MINUTES • MEDIUM

What an amazing salad! It is one of my personal favorites and is a healthy addition to any holiday menu with its festive colors livening up the table. I sometimes replace pomegranate with dried cranberries. If you can find beets that are washed and cooked at your grocery store, it will dramatically reduce your preparation time for this lovely salad. Clementine can be replaced with Kumquats or Blood oranges in season. Always feel free to be creative and make these recipes your own.

SALAD:

1 cup quinoa
2 cups chicken broth
Salt and freshly ground pepper
2 avocados (1½ cups),
    diced and peeled
1 tsp. lemon juice
3 clementines (1 cup),
    peeled and sectioned

2 cups kale, chopped
1 cup pomegranate seeds
    or dried cranberries
3 beets (about 2½ to 3 cups
    cooked), peeled & quartered
¼ cup scallions, chopped

DRESSING:

1 tbsp. clementine juice
    or orange juice

¼ cup pomegranate juice
1 tsp. agave syrup
3 tbsp. olive oil
1 oz. fresh cilantro,
    finely minced
Salt and freshly ground
    pepper to taste
¼ tsp. cumin
2 tsp. clementine rind, grated

1 Using a steamer basket, steam the peeled and cut beets for approximately ½ hour.

2 In a medium saucepan, cook the quinoa according to the package instructions, usually: Bring the broth or water to a boil in a small pan and add the quinoa. Reduce heat and simmer for 15 minutes. Salt and pepper to taste. Reserve and allow to cool.

3 Prepare the dressing in a medium bowl by whisking together the pomegranate juice, oil, clementine or orange juice, agave, cilantro, salt, pepper, cumin and clementine rind. Reserve some cilantro leaves and clementine rind for garnishing.

4 Peel and quarter the avocado adding a little lemon juice to maintain its vibrant color.

5 In a large bowl, combine the avocado, kale, clementine quarters, pomegranates or cranberries, beets and quinoa. Carefully fold in the dressing.

6 Garnish with scallions, clementine rind and cilantro. Serve at room temperature or chilled.

Nutrition Information

| Serving Size **1 Cup** | Servings **10** |

Calories **198**	Potassium . . . . . . **489** mg
Calories from fat **80**	Total Carbohydrates . . . **25** g
Total Fat . . . . **9** g	Dietary Fiber . . . . **8** g
Cholesterol . . . . **0** mg	Sugars . . . . **8** g
Sodium . . . . **86** mg	Protein . . . . **5** g

Vitamin A . . . . **28** %	Folic Acid. . . . . **25** %
Vitamin C . . . . **58** %	Pantothenic Acid. . . . **6** %
Calcium . . . . **5** %	Phosphorus. . . . . . . **13** %
Iron . . . . **9** %	Magnesium. . . . . . . **15** %
Vitamin E. . . . . **8** %	Zinc . . . . **6** %
Vitamin K . . . . . . **134** %	Selenium . . . . **3** %
Vitamin B1. . . . . . . **9** %	Copper. . . . . **21** %
Vitamin B2. . . . . . . **8** %	Manganese . . . . **30** %
Niacin . . . . **6** %	
Vitamin B6. . . . . . . **12** %	

OTHER BENEFICIAL NUTRIENTS (PER SERVING)

Omega-3 (ALA+EPA+DPA+DHA) . . **31** mg
Choline. **23** mg
Beta-Carotene. . . . . **831** mcg
Alpha-Carotene . . . . **13** mcg
Lutein & Zeaxanthin. . . . . **1,220** mcg

Sweet Potato, Apple and Kale Salad with Yellow Raisins

12 CUPS • PREPARATION: 30 MINUTES • COOKING: 30 MINUTES • MEDIUM

This salad is so fresh and delicious! Plus, with kale, apple, raisins and sweet potatoes – the health of this salad speaks for itself. It is so flavorful, you will not believe how healthy it is. If you wish, the millet can be replaced with quinoa.

SALAD:

2 cups chicken or vegetable broth
   or water

1 cup cooked millet or quinoa

2 sweet potatoes, peeled

2 Granny Smith apples, peeled
   and cubed

5 packed cups kale,
   cut in ribbons

1 cup yellow raisins

1 cup pine nuts,
   toasted (optional)

DRESSING:

1 tbsp. Dijon mustard

1 small shallot,
   finely chopped

2 tbsp. apple cider vinegar

½ cup fat-free yogurt

1 tbsp. agave (optional)

2 tbsp. olive oil

Salt and freshly ground
   pepper to taste

1 Cook the millet or quinoa according to the package instructions, usually: Bring the broth or water to a boil in a small pan and add the millet. Reduce heat and simmer for 15 minutes.

2 Toast the pine nuts.

3 Steam the sweet potatoes for 15 minutes in a steam basket.

4 In a large bowl, combine the sweet potatoes, apple, kale, raisins, pine nuts and millet.

5 Combine all the dressing ingredients in a bowl and mix thoroughly.

6 Toss salad with dressing. This salad is great served warm or chilled.

Nutrition Information

Serving Size **1 Cup** Servings **12**

Calories	179	Potassium	428 mg
Calories from fat	24	Total Carbohydrates	34 g
Total Fat	3 g	Dietary Fiber	3 g
Cholesterol	0 mg	Sugars	12 g
Sodium	134 mg	Protein	5 g

Vitamin A	118 %	Folic Acid	7 %
Vitamin C	60 %	Vitamin B12	1 %
Calcium	8 %	Pantothenic Acid	4 %
Iron	8 %	Phosphorus	12 %
Vitamin E	2 %	Magnesium	11 %
Vitamin K	249 %	Zinc	4 %
Vitamin B1	10 %	Selenium	2 %
Vitamin B2	8 %	Copper	32 %
Niacin	8 %	Manganese	30 %
Vitamin B6	12 %		

OTHER BENEFICIAL NUTRIENTS (PER SERVING)

Omega-3 (ALA+EPA+DPA+DHA)	4 mg
Choline	7 mg
Beta-Carotene	3,507 mcg
Alpha-Carotene	17 mcg
Lutein & Zeaxanthin	2,298 mcg

MURIEL AND ANDREW'S TURKEY WITH SPICE RUB

SERVES 12 – 14 PEOPLE • PREPARATION: 30 MINUTES • COOKING: 3 – 3-3/4 HOURS • DIFFICULT

As we prepared this cookbook, I was constantly cooking turkey, so Andrew was eating his Holiday Turkey at least a few times per week for several months. He swore he was going to start gobbling! I sometimes add a bit of turmeric to the rub since that is Andrew's favorite, healthy spice, but this does give the turkey a slightly Eastern flavor. You can always feel free to add your own individual creative touches. I roast my turkey unstuffed, since I feel the stuffing cooks more evenly in a separate pan. Feel free to use your favorite stuffing inside or out, but don't overstuff the bird and remember that a stuffed turkey also takes longer to cook.

1 12–14 lb. turkey, thawed	1 oz. fresh sage	1 tbsp. sweet paprika
6 mini carrots	1 oz. thyme	½ tsp. kosher salt
2 celery stalks	1 bay leaf	¼ tsp. cayenne pepper
4 cups turkey or chicken broth	Black peppercorns	½ tsp. cumin
1 onion, halved	**TURKEY RUB:**	1 tsp. crushed pepper
Dried cloves	1 tbsp. onion powder	1½ tsp. dried thyme
6 garlic cloves	1 tbsp. garlic powder	¼ to ½ cup olive oil

1 Position an oven rack at the lowest level and preheat the oven to 325°. Remove the giblets and neck from inside the turkey and pat dry inside and out. Use a long wooden skewer to secure the neck skin to the back of the turkey. "Clove" your onion by poking a few cloves into each half.

2 In a roasting pan, add the carrots, celery, broth, bay leaf and peppercorns. Then add ½ each of the garlic, "cloved" onion, sage and thyme.

3 Stuff the turkey with the remaining garlic, "cloved" onion, thyme and sage. Secure the legs with string for roasting.

4 Whisk the ingredients for the rub together, gradually adding the olive oil until the mixture becomes a thick paste.

5 Spread half of the rub over the turkey, assuring both top and bottom are coated.

6 Place the turkey breast-side down in the roasting pan. This allows the juices to flow down into the breasts and legs during roasting.

7 Roast turkey for one hour. Remove and cover the turkey with tin foil. Return to oven and roast an additional hour.

8 Remove and flip the turkey breast-side up. Apply the rest of the rub on the top of the bird to create a golden brown color. Cook an additional 90 minutes. If the turkey begins looking too dark, cover with foil.

9 The turkey is done when a cooking thermometer inserted into a thigh registers 165°, approximately 3-3/4 hours total roasting time.

10 When done, remove from the oven. Let the turkey stand for 15 to 20 minutes before transferring to a cutting board for carving.

11 Strain the pan juices in a colander and set aside for the gravy.

12 Serve turkey sliced with Herb and Spice Gravy (Recipe #19).

Nutrition Information

Serving Size **Approx 4 Oz.**   Servings **40**

Calories	140	Potassium	301 mg
Calories from fat	35	Total Carbohydrates	1 g
Total Fat	4 g	Dietary Fiber	0 g
Cholesterol	82 mg	Sugars	0 g
Sodium	215 mg	Protein	25 g

Vitamin A	8 %	Vitamin B6	35 %
Vitamin C	1 %	Folic Acid	3 %
Calcium	2 %	Vitamin B12	23 %
Iron	7 %	Pantothenic Acid	9 %
Vitamin D	3 %	Phosphorus	22 %
Vitamin E	2 %	Magnesium	8 %
Vitamin K	4 %	Zinc	14 %
Vitamin B1	4 %	Selenium	35 %
Vitamin B2	13 %	Copper	5 %
Niacin	44 %	Manganese	3 %

OTHER BENEFICIAL NUTRIENTS (PER SERVING)

Omega-3 (ALA+EPA+DPA+DHA)	95 mg
Choline	67 mg
Beta-Carotene	156 mcg
Alpha-Carotene	58 mcg
Lutein & Zeaxanthin	47 mcg

TURKEY COOKING

Turkey Oven Roasted at 325°F

Type	Weight	Approximate Cooking Time	
		Unstuffed	Stuffed
Turkey (whole)	**8 - 12 lbs.**	2¾ - 3 hours	3 - 3½ hours
Turkey (whole)	**12 - 14 lbs.**	3 - 3¾ hours	3½ - 4 hours
Turkey (whole)	**14 - 18 lbs.**	3¾ - 4¼ hours	4 - 4¼ hours
Turkey (whole)	**18 - 20 lbs.**	4¼ - 4½ hours	4¼ - 4¾ hours
Turkey (whole)	**20 - 24 lbs.**	4½ - 5 hours	4¾ - 5½ hours
Breast (half)	**2 - 3 lbs.**	50 - 60 minutes	
Breast (whole)	**4 - 6 lbs.**	1½ - 2¼ hours	
Breast (whole)	**6 - 8 lbs.**	2¼ - 3¼ hours	
Drumsticks	¾ - 1 lb.	2 - 2¼ hours	
Thighs	¾ - 1 lb.	1¾ - 2 hours	
Wings	6 - 8 oz.	1¾ - 2¼ hours	

Note: Start with turkey at refrigerator temperature. Remove the turkey from the oven when the meat thermometer reads 175° - 180°F; the temperature will continue to rise as the turkey stands.

Grilled Turkey (unstuffed)

Type	Weight	Approximate Cooking Time (internal temperature 180°F)
Turkey (whole) (indirect heat)	**8 - 12 lbs.**	2 - 3 hours
Turkey (whole) (indirect heat)	**12 - 16 lbs.**	3 - 4 hours

Note: When grilling with *Indirect Heat* generally the coals (or burners on a gas grill) are heated to a high heat. When grilling with *Direct Heat* the coals (or burners on a gas grill) are heated to a medium heat. Use these settings unless you have a recipe that states something different.

TOP TURKEY TIPS

Whether you're tackling a Thanksgiving turkey for the first or hundredth time, these tips will ensure your big bird is the best it can be.

1. Thawing a frozen turkey requires patience. The safest method is to thaw turkey in the refrigerator. Be sure to plan ahead — it takes approximately 4–5 days for a 20 pound turkey to fully defrost.

2. For crisper skin, unwrap the turkey the day before roasting and leave it uncovered in the refrigerator overnight.

3. Cooking times will differ depending on whether your bird was purchased fresh or frozen. Plan on 20 minutes per pound in a 350 degree F oven for a defrosted turkey and 10 to 15 minutes per pound for fresh.

4. A turkey will cook more evenly if it is not densely stuffed. Consider adding flavor by loosely filling the cavity with aromatic vegetables — carrots, celery, onion or garlic work nicely — or by carefully tucking fresh herbs underneath the breast skin. For the stuffing lovers, cook the dressing in a casserole dish on the side.

5. Before roasting, coat the outside of the turkey with vegetable or olive oil, season with salt and pepper and tightly cover the breast with aluminum foil to prevent over-browning (it will be removed in step 7).

6. Don't be a peeping tom (no pun intended)! Once you get the turkey in the oven, resist the temptation to open the oven door and admire your handiwork. When the oven temperature fluctuates, you're only increasing the likelihood of a dry bird. About 45 minutes before you think the turkey is done, remove the foil from the breast to allow it to brown.

7. Remove the turkey from the oven and use an instant-read thermometer to determine temperature; it should read 165 degrees F at the thigh when it's done. If you stuff your turkey, check the internal temperature of the stuffing as well; it should be at least 165 degrees.

8. Tent the bird with foil and let rest for about 25 minutes before carving. If you need more time to make gravy, heat up side dishes, etc., you can let the turkey set for up to an hour without losing too much heat.

9. Remember to carve your turkey with a very sharp or electric knife.

TURKEY CABBAGE CUPS
WITH ASIAN DIPPING SAUCE

12 SERVINGS • PREPARATION: 25 MINUTES • COOKING: 12 MINUTES • MEDIUM

I am always trying to come up with new and different ways to use leftover turkey, so I created these Asian-inspired turkey cabbage cups. They are a great way to stay healthy or start a diet the day after the holidays. Andrew likes them so much that I simply use ground turkey to make them throughout the year. Savoy cabbage also works in place of Chinese cabbage, or you may use Bibb lettuce as well.

1 head Chinese cabbage
   (about 12 leaves)

3 tbsp. fresh cilantro, chopped

3 tbsp. fresh mint, chopped

1 cup roasted cashews

¼ cup scallions

1 small jalapeño pepper

2 tbsp. sesame oil

1¼ lbs. ground turkey
   or chopped leftover turkey

1 lime

1 tsp. agave syrup

1 tbsp. fish sauce

DIPPING SAUCE:

¼ cup cashew butter
   or peanut butter

¼ cup light coconut milk

1 tsp. red chili flakes
   (or Sriracha sauce)

3 tbsp. fresh mint, chopped

1 Wash the cabbage leaves and separate; chop the cilantro, mint and cashews; thinly slice the scallions and jalapeño pepper.

2 Make the dipping sauce by whisking all the listed ingredients together: cashew or peanut butter, coconut milk, chili flakes and mint.

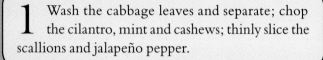

3 Heat sesame oil in large skillet over medium heat. If using ground turkey, brown for approximately 10 minutes or until cooked through. If using leftover turkey, warm for 5 minutes.

4 Combine the turkey with the cilantro, mint, lime juice, agave, fish sauce and cashews. Cook together for about 2 more minutes so the flavors mix well.

5 Wrap a generous serving of the turkey mixture in a single cabbage or lettuce leaf and garnish with scallions and a slice of jalapeno pepper. Serve with the dipping sauce on the side.

Nutrition Information

Serving Size **1 Turkey Cabbage Cup**   Servings **12**

Calories **181**	Potassium . . . . . . **396 mg**
Calories from fat **99**	Total Carbohydrates . . . . **7 g**
Total Fat . . . . **11 g**	Dietary Fiber . . . . . . **1 g**
Cholesterol . . . . . . **42 mg**	Sugars . . . . **2 g**
Sodium . . . . **206 mg**	Protein . . . . **14 g**

Vitamin A . . . . **66 %**	Vitamin B6 . . . . **19 %**
Vitamin C . . . . **59 %**	Folic Acid . . . . **16 %**
Calcium . . . . **10 %**	Vitamin B12 . . . . . **11 %**
Iron . . . . **12 %**	Pantothenic Acid . . . . **8 %**
Vitamin D . . . . **2 %**	Phosphorus . . . . **20 %**
Vitamin E . . . . **2 %**	Magnesium . . . . **15 %**
Vitamin K . . . . **40 %**	Zinc . . . . **15 %**
Vitamin B1 . . . . **6 %**	Selenium . . . . **18 %**
Vitamin B2 . . . . . . **11 %**	Copper . . . . **17 %**
Niacin . . . . **18 %**	Manganese . . . . **12 %**

OTHER BENEFICIAL NUTRIENTS (PER SERVING)

Omega-3 (ALA+EPA+DPA+DHA) . . **82 mg**	
Choline . . . . **42 mg**	
Beta-Carotene . . . . **1,923 mcg**	
Alpha-Carotene . . . . **1 mcg**	
Lutein & Zeaxanthin . . . . **97 mcg**	

Suzette's Turkey Loaf

10 SLICES • PREPARATION: 20 MINUTES • COOKING: 50 MINUTES • EASY

My girlfriend, Suzette, made me this delicious Turkey Loaf one evening and I had four helpings! Of course, we completely lost track of how many servings Andrew had. I have added a few of my own twists such as chopped mushrooms and replaced the breadcrumbs with oat bran (or cooked quinoa). It has become a year-round favorite at the house and it is so easy to make! I generally serve it with a side of green beans and a salad.

1½ lbs. lean ground turkey

1 cup Parmesan cheese,
　　divided into two ½ cups

8 oz. mushrooms, finely chopped

¾ cup oat bran

3 cloves garlic, minced

2 shallots or 1 large red onion,
　　chopped

A few sprigs of parsley, minced

1 cup organic ketchup,
　　divided into two ½ cups

4 egg whites (or 2 whole eggs)

2 tbsp. Worcestershire sauce

½ cup turkey or
　　chicken broth

Salt and freshly ground
　　pepper to taste

1 tbsp. olive oil

1 Preheat oven to 350°. In a large bowl, mix the turkey, ½ cup Parmesan cheese, mushrooms, oat bran, shallots, garlic, parsley, ½ cup ketchup, Worcestershire sauce, eggs, salt and pepper. Increase moisture by adding broth as needed. (I mix the whole thing with my hands!)

2 Grease a loaf pan with the olive oil and evenly spread the turkey mixture into it.

3 Cover turkey loaf with the remaining ketchup and Parmesan cheese.

4 Bake for 45 to 50 minutes.

5 Slice and serve with a side salad.

Nutrition Information

Serving Size **1 Slice (3 oz.)**   Servings **10**

Calories	189	Potassium	374 mg
Calories from fat	72	Total Carbohydrates	14 g
Total Fat	8 g	Dietary Fiber	2 g
Cholesterol	39 mg	Sugars	7 g
Sodium	257 mg	Protein	16 g

Vitamin A	5 %	Vitamin B6	13 %
Vitamin C	4 %	Folic Acid	4 %
Calcium	13 %	Vitamin B12	11 %
Iron	8 %	Pantothenic Acid	10 %
Vitamin D	2 %	Phosphorus	24 %
Vitamin E	4 %	Magnesium	10 %
Vitamin K	2 %	Zinc	12 %
Vitamin B1	10 %	Selenium	27 %
Vitamin B2	20 %	Copper	10 %
Niacin	20 %	Manganese	24 %

OTHER BENEFICIAL NUTRIENTS (PER SERVING)

Omega-3 (ALA+EPA+DPA+DHA)	74 mg
Choline	36 mg
Beta-Carotene	81 mcg
Lutein & Zeaxanthin	36 mcg
Lycopene	3,434 mcg

MIRIAM'S TURKEY TACOS

15 SMALL TACOS • PREPARATION: 30 MINUTES • COOKING: 12 MINUTES • MEDIUM

Miriam works with us in the kitchen and she is an absolute wizard with cooking knives! She also has her own tortilla press and taught me how to make my own homemade Turkey Tacos. The homemade tortillas are amazing, but no need to worry, since I normally use store-bought gluten-free tortillas. Not everyone has the special press or the time! I usually serve these tacos with black beans, brown rice, homemade guacamole and Pico de Gallo or salsa.

GUACAMOLE:

2 ripe avocados

⅔ cup cherry tomatoes, chopped

1 small shallot, chopped

2 cloves garlic, minced

½ jalapeño pepper, chopped

A few leaves of Cilantro, minced

1 lime, juiced

TURKEY TACOS:

1½ lbs. ground turkey or chopped leftover turkey

1 tsp. canola oil

1 small red onion, chopped

2 cloves garlic, minced

1 tsp. cumin

1½ tsp. Mexican Fiesta spice (or chili powder)

1 tsp. dried oregano

Salt and freshly ground pepper

15 small gluten-free tortillas

¼ head red cabbage, minced

4 oz. queso fresco, crumbled

⅓ cup sour cream (optional)

Fresh cilantro

½ jalapeño, thinly sliced

1 lime, thinly sliced

1 Cut the avocado in half to seed and peel. Add the cherry tomatoes, shallots, garlic, jalapeño, minced cilantro and lime juice.

2 Mash and mix ingredients to make the guacamole. Cover with plastic wrap and refrigerate.

3 In a large skillet over medium heat, cook the turkey in canola oil with the onion, garlic, cumin, Mexican Fiesta Spice, oregano, salt and pepper. Cook 10 to 12 minutes for ground turkey, 5 minutes for leftover turkey.

4 Warm tortillas one at a time in a small skillet and wrap in tin foil to keep warm and fresh.

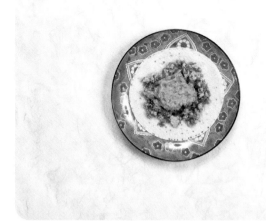

5 In each tortilla, place 1/3 cup of the turkey mix and a spoonful of guacamole.

6 Garnish with red cabbage, queso fresco, sour cream (optional), cilantro, and a slice each of jalapeño and lime. Yum!

Nutrition Information

Serving Size **1 Taco**   Servings **15**

Calories	**224**	Potassium	**356 mg**
Calories from fat	**98**	Total Carbohydrates	**19 g**
Total Fat	**11 g**	Dietary Fiber	**6 g**
Cholesterol	**36 mg**	Sugars	**3 g**
Sodium	**252 mg**	Protein	**13 g**

Vitamin A	**8 %**	Vitamin B6	**16 %**
Vitamin C	**26 %**	Folic Acid	**16 %**
Calcium	**8 %**	Vitamin B12	**10 %**
Iron	**11 %**	Pantothenic Acid	**9 %**
Vitamin D	**3 %**	Phosphorus	**18 %**
Vitamin E	**4 %**	Magnesium	**7 %**
Vitamin K	**18 %**	Zinc	**11 %**
Vitamin B1	**13 %**	Selenium	**23 %**
Vitamin B2	**11 %**	Copper	**8 %**
Niacin	**20 %**	Manganese	**13 %**

OTHER BENEFICIAL NUTRIENTS (PER SERVING)

Omega-3 (ALA+EPA+DPA+DHA)	**105 mg**
Choline	**35 mg**
Beta-Carotene	**192 mcg**
Alpha-Carotene	**19 mcg**
Lutein & Zeaxanthin	**143 mcg**
Lycopene	**172 mcg**

WHOLE SALMON FILLET
WITH CILANTRO AND PISTACHIO PESTO

8 SERVINGS • PREPARATION: 20 MINUTES • COOKING: 25 – 30 MINUTES • MEDIUM

I liked the idea of a whole salmon fillet during the holidays as the presentation is amazing and it is so delicious and full of healthy Omega-3 Oils! Andrew and I really welcome it as a change from all the turkey we seem to eat during the Holidays. It is also a great opportunity to offer something different if you have guests visiting for awhile over the holidays. We don't like to overcook our salmon, but feel free to cook it a little longer to satisfy your individual taste.

1 whole salmon fillet (3-5 lbs.), deboned

¼ cup pine nuts

¼ cup unsalted pistachios, shelled

2 limes

2 tbsp. olive oil

1 oz. cilantro

1 garlic clove

¼ cup water

1 tbsp. agave syrup

Freshly ground pepper to taste

1 Preheat oven to 350°. Roast the pine nuts and pistachios in a pan for 5 minutes.

2 Make the pesto in a mini blender by mixing the pistachios, pine nuts, the juice of 1 lime, 1 tbsp. olive oil, half the cilantro and the garlic. Blend well adding water for the desired consistency. Reserve.

3 In a small mixing bowl, combine the juice of one lime, 1 tbsp. olive oil, agave syrup and pepper. Place salmon on a baking tray lined with foil and coat the top of the fillet with the mixture.

4 Add the pesto to the top of fillet as pictured. Garnish with the remaining cilantro. Bake for approximately 25 minutes until color changes.

5 Serve directly from the oven with a side salad or a quinoa dish.

Nutrition Information

Serving Size **8 Oz.**   Servings **8**

Calories	**213**	Potassium	**498 mg**
Calories from fat	**121**	Total Carbohydrates	**5 g**
Total Fat	**13 g**	Dietary Fiber	**1 g**
Cholesterol	**47 mg**	Sugars	**3 g**
Sodium	**38 mg**	Protein	**18 g**

Vitamin A	**1 %**	Folic Acid	**7 %**
Vitamin C	**6 %**	Vitamin B12	**45 %**
Calcium	**2 %**	Pantothenic Acid	**15 %**
Iron	**6 %**	Phosphorus	**22 %**
Vitamin E	**5 %**	Magnesium	**10 %**
Vitamin K	**3 %**	Zinc	**6 %**
Vitamin B1	**16 %**	Selenium	**45 %**
Vitamin B2	**20 %**	Copper	**16 %**
Niacin	**35 %**	Manganese	**22 %**
Vitamin B6	**39 %**		

OTHER BENEFICIAL NUTRIENTS (PER SERVING)

Omega-3 (ALA+EPA+DPA+DHA)	**1,469 mg**
Choline	**3 mg**
Beta–Carotene	**23 mcg**
Lutein & Zeaxanthin	**57 mcg**

MURIEL'S KALE, RICOTTA AND PUMPKIN LASAGNA

12 SERVINGS • PREPARATION: 30 MINUTES • COOKING: 45 - 60 MINUTES • MEDIUM

This is the most delicious lasagna ever! I cannot leave it on the kitchen counter or Andrew makes it disappear. Totally vegetarian and incredibly healthy! It pleases everyone! Ricotta is a very light cheese, so the calories are much lower than normal lasagna. I use "oven-ready" lasagna noodles, which reduces the cooking time of this recipe to 45 minutes. We use gluten-free, but feel free to use your favorite type of noodles and increase the cooking time to an hour if using an uncooked variety.

1 15 oz. container ricotta cheese

2 cups fresh kale, washed and finely chopped

1 oz. basil minced or in Chiffonade

2 cloves garlic, minced

3 cups Monterey Jack cheese

3 whole eggs or 5 egg whites, beaten

½ tsp. red chili flakes (optional)

Salt and freshly ground pepper to taste

1 15 oz. can pure pumpkin (not pie mix)

1 tsp. pumpkin spice

1 15 oz. jar marinara sauce

1 tsp. olive oil

8 lasagna noodles (I use gluten-free, "oven-ready" noodles)

1 Preheat oven to 375°. In a bowl, combine the ricotta, kale, basil, garlic, eggs, ¾ cup Monterey Jack cheese, chili flakes, and a dash of salt and pepper. Mix with a fork or in a blender and set aside.

2 In another bowl, mix together the pumpkin, pumpkin spice, a pinch of salt and pepper and the marinara sauce.

3 In a greased lasagna pan, layer the lasagna in the following order: Pumpkin-marinara sauce and Monterey Jack cheese, 2 lasagna noodles, ricotta-kale mixture and 2 more noodles. Repeat.

4 Top with a light covering of ricotta-kale, pumpkin-marinara sauce and remaining Monterey Jack cheese.

5 Bake, covered with foil, for 40 minutes until the noodles are al dente. Remove foil and bake 5 more minutes for a nice crust. Let it cool a half hour before you slice and serve.

Nutrition Information

Serving Size **1 Slice (6 Oz.)**   Servings **12**

Calories	230	Potassium	238 mg
Calories from fat	130	Total Carbohydrates	10 g
Total Fat	14 g	Dietary Fiber	0 g
Cholesterol	44 mg	Sugars	2 g
Sodium	229 mg	Protein	15 g

Vitamin A	158 %	Vitamin B6	6 %
Vitamin C	26 %	Folic Acid	7 %
Calcium	32 %	Vitamin B12	7 %
Iron	8 %	Pantothenic Acid	4 %
Vitamin D	2 %	Phosphorus	22 %
Vitamin E	3 %	Magnesium	8 %
Vitamin K	121 %	Zinc	10 %
Vitamin B1	4 %	Selenium	18 %
Vitamin B2	19 %	Copper	13 %
Niacin	3 %	Manganese	11 %

OTHER BENEFICIAL NUTRIENTS (PER SERVING)

Choline	15 mg
Beta-Carotene	3,569 mcg
Alpha-Carotene	1,925 mcg
Lutein & Zeaxanthin	1,067 mcg
Lycopene	36 mcg

HERB AND SPICE GRAVY

ABOUT 3 1/2 CUPS • PREPARATION: 5 MINUTES • COOKING: 10 MINUTES • EASY

This is actually a roux made with the juices from my roasted turkey. Much of the flavoring will come from the spices contained in the juices. It's a very simple and flexible recipe. You can add almost anything you wish such as sautéed mushrooms, onions, additional herbs, a little cream or even some Madeira. I usually sauté my onions or mushrooms first in a little butter to give them an extra flavor boost. Andrew's mother uses cornstarch to thicken her gravy, but we prefer to use Garbanzo flour; however, any flour will work.

4 tbsp. butter

½ cup garbanzo flour

3 cups of turkey broth from
    Turkey with Spice Rub
    (Recipe #13)

1 sprig of thyme

A few sage leaves, minced

Salt and freshly ground
    pepper to taste

1 Make a roux by melting the butter in a small saucepan, adding flour and whisking constantly until a thick paste is formed.

2 Slowly add the broth continuing to whisk constantly until you achieve the desired consistency.

3 Add the herbs, and salt and pepper to taste. Serve hot. I like to garnish it with festive red peppercorns!

Nutrition Information

Serving Size **1/4 Cup**   Servings **14**

Calories	64	Potassium	45 mg
Calories from fat	44	Total Carbohydrates	4 g
Total Fat	5 g	Dietary Fiber	0 g
Cholesterol	13 mg	Sugars	0 g
Sodium	163 mg	Protein	1 g

Vitamin A	3 %	Copper	1 %
Calcium	1 %	Manganese	2 %
Iron	1 %		
Vitamin D	1 %		
Vitamin E	1 %		
Vitamin K	1 %		
Vitamin B2	1 %		
Niacin	2 %		
Vitamin B12	1 %		
Phosphorus	1 %		

OTHER BENEFICIAL NUTRIENTS (PER SERVING)

Omega-3 (ALA+EPA+DPA+DHA)	19 mg
Choline	3 mg
Beta-Carotene	10 mcg

FRESH CRANBERRY SAUCE WITH DRIED FIGS AND MINT

2 CUPS • PREPARATION: 10 MINUTES • COOKING: 10 MINUTES • EASY

There are so many standard ways to serve cranberry sauce that I was looking for something a little different, so I combined the cranberries with dried figs, some orange juice and fresh mint. When they are all combined and cooked, the sauce takes on a wonderfully delicious jam-like quality. Of course, since cranberries can be tart, you can always add a little more agave syrup or honey if you want a sweeter version. I sometimes use this sauce over pancakes for breakfast or on our Turkey Tacos (Recipe #16) the day after a holiday dinner. It also refrigerates well.

1 12 oz. bag of fresh cranberries	1 lb. dried figs, quartered
½ cup orange juice	1 oz. fresh mint leaves, minced
¼ cup agave syrup or honey	Zest of 1 orange

1 In a saucepan or skillet, combine the cranberries with the orange juice and agave. Cook uncovered over medium heat for approximately 5 minutes until most of the cranberries pop open and the mixture thickens.

2 Add the dried figs and continue to cook over medium heat for an additional 5 to 7 minutes.

3 Remove from heat. Add the fresh minced mint and orange zest, mixing well. Refrigerate until cool (preferably overnight). Serve with turkey.

Nutrition Information

Serving Size **2 Tablespoons**   Servings **16**

Calories	112	Potassium	240 mg
Calories from fat	3	Total Carbohydrates	26 g
Total Fat	0 g	Dietary Fiber	4 g
Cholesterol	0 mg	Sugars	20 g
Sodium	4 mg	Protein	1 g
Vitamin A	2 %	Folic Acid	2 %
Vitamin C	13 %	Pantothenic Acid	2 %
Calcium	5 %	Phosphorus	2 %
Iron	5 %	Magnesium	6 %
Vitamin E	2 %	Zinc	1 %
Vitamin K	7 %	Copper	5 %
Vitamin B1	2 %	Manganese	13 %
Vitamin B2	2 %		
Niacin	1 %		
Vitamin B6	3 %		

OTHER BENEFICIAL NUTRIENTS (PER SERVING)

Choline	4 mg
Beta-Carotene	15 mcg
Lutein & Zeaxanthin	29 mcg

CORNBREAD, TURKEY SAUSAGE AND PECAN STUFFING

20 SERVINGS · PREPARATION: 30 MINUTES · COOKING: 45 MINUTES · MEDIUM

This cornbread stuffing is made with our Simple and Easy Cornbread (Recipe #24). The flavors mix well and make it the perfect holiday stuffing. I like to use apple-turkey sausage because I think its sweetness and spices go great with cornbread, but you can feel free to use your own favorite. I also typically make the cornbread a day ahead to save time (which can be dangerous if Andrew gets his hands on it). Actually, this entire recipe can be made a day ahead and refrigerated, ready to bake.

2 tbsp. olive oil	½ oz. fresh thyme	3 large eggs, beaten
2 shallots, chopped (1 cup)	½ oz. fresh sage	½ cup low-sodium turkey or chicken broth
2 cloves garlic, minced	1 cup roasted pecans, chopped	
1 cup celery, chopped	Salt and freshly ground pepper to taste	4 cups Cornbread (Recipe #24)
4 turkey sausages		

1 Preheat oven to 375°. Heat 1 tbsp. olive oil in a large skillet over medium heat. Sauté shallots, garlic and celery for approximately 10 minutes.

2 Pierce the sausages with a fork and sauté in a small skillet for approximately 4 minutes on each side depending on their size.

3 Cut the cooked sausages into small pieces and add to the large skillet with the vegetables along with the thyme, sage, pecans, salt and pepper. Sauté for 5 additional minutes.

4 In a small bowl whisk the eggs with the broth. In a large bowl toss the cornbread with the vegetables and the egg/broth mixture. If it seems too dry, add a little extra broth.

5 Place the final mixture in a casserole dish greased with a little olive oil or butter.

6 Bake for 40 to 45 minutes. Unbaked stuffing can be refrigerated overnight and cooked the next day for convenience.

Nutrition Information

Serving Size **1/2 Cup**   Servings **20**

Calories **173**	Potassium . . . . . . **336 mg**
Calories from fat **94**	Total Carbohydrates . . . **13 g**
Total Fat . . . . **10 g**	Dietary Fiber . . . . **2 g**
Cholesterol . . . . . . **71 mg**	Sugars . . . . **3 g**
Sodium . . . . **329 mg**	Protein . . . . **6 g**

Vitamin A . . . . **5 %**	Vitamin B6. . . . . **8 %**
Vitamin C . . . . **3 %**	Folic Acid. . . . . **4 %**
Calcium . . . . **5 %**	Vitamin B12. . . . . . . **6 %**
Iron . . . . **6 %**	Pantothenic Acid . . . . **5 %**
Vitamin D . . . . **4 %**	Phosphorus. . . . . . . **22 %**
Vitamin E. . . . . **3 %**	Magnesium. . . . . **8 %**
Vitamin K . . . . **5 %**	Zinc . . . . **8 %**
Vitamin B1 . . . . **7 %**	Selenium . . . . **10 %**
Vitamin B2. . . . . . . **10 %**	Copper. . . . . **6 %**
Niacin . . . . **5 %**	Manganese . . . . **18 %**

OTHER BENEFICIAL NUTRIENTS (PER SERVING)

Omega-3 (ALA+EPA+DPA+DHA). .	**53 mg**
Choline.	**54 mg**
Beta-Carotene	**42 mcg**
Alpha-Carotene	**8 mcg**
Lutein & Zeaxanthin	**239 mcg**
Lycopene.	**1 mcg**

WILD RICE STUFFING
WITH CRANBERRIES AND CHESTNUTS

20 SERVINGS • PREPARATION: 30 MINUTES • COOKING: 60 MINUTES • MEDIUM

We love the delicious, healthy holiday flavors of this stuffing. I was looking for an alternative to the typical bread stuffing and since we try to eat gluten-free, the wild rice is a nice option with the chestnuts adding a rich, nutty taste. The cranberries can be replaced with dried figs or dried apricots. Either way, it will be lovely and delicious. Enjoy!

4 cups chicken broth

1 tbsp. + 1 tsp. olive oil

2 cups wild rice

1½ cup dried cranberries

2 shallots (1 cup), chopped

3 cloves garlic, minced

1½ cup carrots, chopped

1½ cup celery, chopped

1½ cup roasted chestnuts chopped

1 sprig of thyme

Salt and freshly ground
pepper to taste

½ oz. fresh sage

1 Preheat oven to 375°. In a saucepan bring broth and 1 tsp. of olive oil to a boil. Add rice and cook according to package instructions (usually cover and let simmer for 40 minutes).

2 Add the cranberries to the rice for the last 10 minutes of cooking.

3 In a large skillet over medium heat, combine the remaining olive oil with the shallots, garlic, carrots and celery. Sauté for approximately 15 minutes until the vegetables are tender.

4 Add the chestnuts, salt and pepper, thyme and sage to the vegetables.

5 Mix seasoned vegetables together with the rice and cranberries. Pour the combined mixture into a baking dish adding the remaining ½ cup of broth. You may add additional broth if mixture appears dry.

6 Bake for approximately 20 minutes. Serve hot.

Nutrition Information

Serving Size **1/2 Cup**   Servings **20**

Calories	**97**	Potassium	**136 mg**
Calories from fat	**12**	Total Carbohydrates	**19 g**
Total Fat	**1 g**	Dietary Fiber	**2 g**
Cholesterol	**0 mg**	Sugars	**8 g**
Sodium	**98 mg**	Protein	**2 g**

Vitamin A	**33 %**	Pantothenic Acid	**2 %**
Vitamin C	**8 %**	Phosphorus	**4 %**
Calcium	**2 %**	Magnesium	**3 %**
Iron	**3 %**	Zinc	**3 %**
Vitamin E	**2 %**	Selenium	**1 %**
Vitamin B1	**3 %**	Copper	**6 %**
Vitamin B2	**3 %**	Manganese	**14 %**
Niacin	**4 %**		
Vitamin B6	**7 %**		
Folic Acid	**5 %**		

OTHER BENEFICIAL NUTRIENTS (PER SERVING)

Omega-3 (ALA+EPA+DPA+DHA)	**7 mg**
Choline	**6 mg**
Beta-Carotene	**821 mcg**
Alpha-Carotene	**334 mcg**
Lutein & Zeaxanthin	**64 mcg**

QUINOA CASSEROLE WITH COLLARD GREENS, CHERRIES AND ALMONDS

16 SERVINGS • PREPARATION: 25 MINUTES • COOKING: 35 MINUTES • MEDIUM

Since Andrew and I do not normally eat white rice, pasta, potatoes or bread at home, we are always seeking more nutritious, healthier alternatives. Quinoa is not a grain, but rather a seed that comes from a plant closely related to spinach. Collard greens are a cruciferous vegetable - another healthy, nutritious alternative. The addition of dried cherries gives this casserole a delectable sweetness to go with its wonderful texture and abundance of healthy nutrients.

2 cups quinoa

4 cups broth (preferably turkey)

Salt and freshly ground
    pepper to taste

1 cup sliced almonds

1 leek, chopped (1 cup)

1 tbsp. olive oil

4 cups (7 oz.) collard greens
    minced in thin ribbons

2 cloves garlic, minced

1 cup dried cherries

Few sprigs fresh thyme,
    chopped

1 tsp. allspice

1 Preheat oven to 375°. Cook the quinoa according to the package instructions, usually: Bring the broth or water to a boil in a medium pan and add the quinoa. Reduce heat and simmer for 15 minutes.

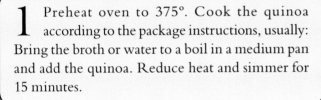

2 In a small sauté pan, toast the almonds over low heat for 5 minutes.

3 In a skillet over medium heat, sauté the leek in olive oil for approximately 5 minutes.

4 Add the collard greens and garlic, cooking for an additional 5 minutes and then stir in the cooked quinoa, cherries, toasted almonds, salt, pepper, thyme and allspice.

5 Place the mixture in a casserole, lightly coated with olive oil and bake for 15 to 20 minutes.

Nutrition Information

Serving Size **1/2 Cup**   Servings **16**

Calories	**139**	Potassium	**265 mg**
Calories from fat	**46**	Total Carbohydrates	**18 g**
Total Fat	**5 g**	Dietary Fiber	**7 g**
Cholesterol	**0 mg**	Sugars	**2 g**
Sodium	**143 mg**	Protein	**6 g**

Vitamin A	**11 %**	Folic Acid	**15 %**
Vitamin C	**8 %**	Vitamin B12	**1 %**
Calcium	**6 %**	Pantothenic Acid	**3 %**
Iron	**8 %**	Phosphorus	**14 %**
Vitamin E	**12 %**	Magnesium	**16 %**
Vitamin K	**53 %**	Zinc	**7 %**
Vitamin B1	**7 %**	Selenium	**3 %**
Vitamin B2	**9 %**	Copper	**11 %**
Niacin	**5 %**	Manganese	**35 %**
Vitamin B6	**8 %**		

OTHER BENEFICIAL NUTRIENTS (PER SERVING)

Omega-3 (ALA+EPA+DPA+DHA)	**32 mg**
Choline	**28 mg**
Beta-Carotene	**330 mcg**
Alpha-Carotene	**1 mcg**
Lutein & Zeaxanthin	**538 mcg**

SIMPLE AND EASY CORNBREAD

15 SERVINGS • PREPARATION: 20 MINUTES • COOKING: 25 MINUTES • MEDIUM

If you are making this cornbread for stuffing, the most difficult part of the recipe will be to keep everyone from eating it beforehand! It is only safe, if I know Andrew is not around. I almost always make my own cornbread, but if you would rather use a "package mix," Bob's Red Mill® makes a great, gluten-free version and Pamela's® Cornbread & Muffin Mix works very well too. You will notice that ours contains little to no added sugar or fat.

1¾ cups cornmeal (stoneground)

1 tbsp. baking powder

1 tsp. baking soda

1 tsp. salt

2 eggs, beaten

4 tbsp. melted butter

1 cup fat-free buttermilk

⅔ cup skim milk

1 tbsp. honey

1 Preheat oven to 450°. In a medium bowl, combine the cornmeal, baking powder, baking soda and salt.

2 In a small bowl, combine the eggs, melted butter, buttermilk, skim milk and honey.

3 Quickly whisk the wet ingredients into the dry being careful not to over mix.

4 Pour the batter into a buttered dish and bake for 20 to 25 minutes until lightly brown on the top and a knife (or toothpick) comes out dry. Carefully cut and serve.

Nutrition Information

Serving Size **1 Slice**   Servings **15**

Calories	113	Potassium	300 mg
Calories from fat	42	Total Carbohydrates	14 g
Total Fat	5 g	Dietary Fiber	1 g
Cholesterol	46 mg	Sugars	3 g
Sodium	309 mg	Protein	3 g

Vitamin A	4 %	Vitamin B12	3 %
Calcium	4 %	Pantothenic Acid	3 %
Iron	4 %	Phosphorus	22 %
Vitamin D	3 %	Magnesium	6 %
Vitamin E	1 %	Zinc	3 %
Vitamin B1	5 %	Selenium	9 %
Vitamin B2	7 %	Copper	2 %
Niacin	3 %	Manganese	4 %
Vitamin B6	3 %		
Folic Acid	2 %		

OTHER BENEFICIAL NUTRIENTS (PER SERVING)

Omega-3 (ALA+EPA+DPA+DHA)	25 mg
Choline	38 mg
Beta-Carotene	20 mcg
Alpha-Carotene	9 mcg
Lutein & Zeaxanthin	243 mcg

GREEN BEANS AMANDINE
WITH MISO PASTE

8 SERVINGS • PREPARATION: 10 MINUTES • COOKING: 13 MINUTES • EASY

Green Beans are a classic Thanksgiving and holiday dish and are a delicious way to eat your very nutritious greens. I've added a twist by using white miso paste, which imparts a delicious Asian flair that is a real crowd-pleaser and goes well with the almonds. Taste the dish before adding any salt as the miso paste already imparts a subtle salty flavor.

2 lbs. green beans (ends removed)

1½ tbsp. white miso paste

¼ cup hot water

1 tbsp. coconut oil

¾ cup slivered almonds

Freshly ground pepper to taste

1 tsp. red chili flakes

1 Bring water to a boil in a steamer basket and steam the green beans for 5 minutes until bright green, crisp and tender.

2 Dissolve the miso paste in the hot water.

3 In a large skillet, melt the coconut oil over medium heat, add the miso paste and almonds, and cook for approximately 3 minutes.

4 Add the steamed green beans to the skillet and cook for an additional 5 minutes.

5 Garnish with the pepper and chili flakes before serving.

Nutrition Information

Serving Size **1 Cup**   Servings **8**

Calories	104	Potassium	188 mg
Calories from fat	63	Total Carbohydrates	7 g
Total Fat	7 g	Dietary Fiber	3 g
Cholesterol	0 mg	Sugars	2 g
Sodium	123 mg	Protein	3 g

Vitamin A	9 %	Folic Acid	6 %
Vitamin C	10 %	Pantothenic Acid	2 %
Calcium	5 %	Phosphorus	7 %
Iron	6 %	Magnesium	10 %
Vitamin E	15 %	Zinc	3 %
Vitamin K	9 %	Selenium	1 %
Vitamin B1	4 %	Copper	7 %
Vitamin B2	10 %	Manganese	19 %
Niacin	4 %		
Vitamin B6	5 %		

OTHER BENEFICIAL NUTRIENTS (PER SERVING)

Choline	15 mg
Beta-Carotene	240 mcg
Alpha-Carotene	35 mcg
Lutein & Zeaxanthin	350 mcg

PURPLE CAULIFLOWER
WITH DATES AND PINE NUTS

8 SERVINGS • PREPARATION: 15 MINUTES • COOKING: 20 MINUTES • EASY

We love cauliflower in every color and shape at our house. It's a healthy cruciferous vegetable and the more colorful varieties are even richer in protective compounds. I like to use purple or green cauliflower for this recipe, but any type will work. I've found that uniformly slicing the cauliflower cooks more evenly and makes for a lovely presentation!

2 tbsp. olive oil

2 heads of cauliflower, sliced

1 tsp. garlic powder

1 tsp. onion powder

Salt and freshly ground
pepper to taste

¾ cup dates, chopped

¾ cup pine nuts

1 Preheat oven to 375°. Prepare a baking sheet with foil and coat with half of the olive oil. Spread cauliflower slices on the sheet sprinkling with garlic and onion powder. Add salt and pepper to taste. Bake for 15 minutes.

2 Toast the pine nuts in a small skillet for 5 minutes on low heat.

3 Turn the cauliflower over with tongs.

4 Add the dates and pine nuts to the cauliflower and roast for an additional 10 minutes.

5 Serve hot as a side dish.

Nutrition Information

Serving Size **1 Cup**		Servings **8**

Calories **212**	Potassium . . . . . . **613 mg**
Calories from fat . . . **112**	Total Carbohydrates . . . **20 g**
Total Fat . . . . **12 g**	Dietary Fiber . . . . **3 g**
Cholesterol . . . . . . **0 mg**	Sugars . . . . **12 g**
Sodium . . . . **45 mg**	Protein . . . . **5 g**

Vitamin C . . . . . . **118 %**	Pantothenic Acid . . . **11 %**
Calcium . . . . **4 %**	Phosphorus . . . . **15 %**
Iron . . . . **8 %**	Magnesium. . . . . . . **15 %**
Vitamin E. . . . . **9 %**	Zinc . . . . **9 %**
Vitamin K . . . . **28 %**	Selenium . . . . **2 %**
Vitamin B1 . . . . **9 %**	Copper . . . . **13 %**
Vitamin B2 . . . . **8 %**	Manganese . . . . **69 %**
Niacin . . . . **7 %**	
Vitamin B6 . . . . **16 %**	
Folic Acid . . . . **22 %**	

OTHER BENEFICIAL NUTRIENTS (PER SERVING)

Omega-3 (ALA+EPA+DPA+DHA) . . **40 mg**
Choline. . . . . **73 mg**
Beta-Carotene. . . . . **3 mcg**
Lutein & Zeaxanthin. . . . . **13 mcg**

ANDREW'S MASHED CAULIFLOWER

8 SERVINGS • PREPARATION: 5 MINUTES • COOKING: 15 MINUTES • EASY

Andrew loves his mashed potatoes. At family gatherings he remains the "official mashed potato maker;" but, other than holidays, he does not consume them and in recent years, he has gotten everyone to try our Mashed Cauliflower. This recipe originates from Andrew's desire to find a delicious, healthy and nutritious alternative to his mashed potatoes without the high calories, carbs and fat. This recipe is a healthy treat that is exceptionally low in calories and full of protective phytonutrients. You can also add your favorite herbs, spices or condiments to expand the flavor possibilities. Like Andrew, you will be astounded how much you will enjoy this healthy alternative to mashed potatoes.

---

2 heads (3 lbs.) cauliflower	1½ cups vegetable broth
1 tbsp. butter	Salt and pepper to taste
2 tbsp. almond meal	Sprigs of rosemary for garnish

1 Wash the cauliflower and separate the florets. Steam for 15 minutes.

2 Put the cauliflower in the blender with the butter, almond meal and broth. Mix well until pureed (approximately 2 minutes).

3 Add salt and pepper to taste, and serve in individual bowls decorated with rosemary.

Nutrition Information

Serving Size **1 Cup**   Servings **8**

Calories	78	Potassium	534 mg
Calories from fat	33	Total Carbohydrates	10 g
Total Fat	4 g	Dietary Fiber	2 g
Cholesterol	4 mg	Sugars	4 g
Sodium	240 mg	Protein	4 g

Vitamin A	1 %	Vitamin B6	16 %
Vitamin C	137 %	Folic Acid	25 %
Calcium	5 %	Pantothenic Acid	12 %
Iron	5 %	Phosphorus	9 %
Vitamin E	5 %	Magnesium	9 %
Vitamin K	33 %	Zinc	8 %
Vitamin B1	6 %	Selenium	7 %
Vitamin B2	9 %	Copper	2 %
Niacin	5 %	Manganese	4 %

OTHER BENEFICIAL NUTRIENTS (PER SERVING)

Choline	6 mg
Beta-Carotene	20 mcg

CAULIFLOWER CASSEROLE
DE MA GRAND-MÈRE

7 SERVINGS • PREPARATION: 20 MINUTES • COOKING: 15 MINUTES • DIFFICULT

My grandmother used to make this as a special treat for me when I was a child. I loved it then and I love it now. Who knew back then how healthy and nutritious cauliflower was? It is such a pleasure to see Andrew now enjoy my Grand-Mère's delicious and nutritious cauliflower casserole. In fact, it is so rich and delicious that Andrew still does not believe how low it is in calories.

1 head (1½ lbs.) cauliflower	1½ cups warm skim milk
3 tbsp. butter	1 cup Swiss cheese
¼ cup garbanzo flour (or regular flour)	Salt and pepper to taste
	1 pinch nutmeg

1 Preheat the oven to 375°. Wash the cauliflower and prepare the florets. Steam for 10 minutes with a little salt. You can also cook them in boiling water, but drain them well.

2 While the cauliflower is cooking, make the Béchamel sauce. In a small saucepan, melt 2 tbsp. butter over medium heat. Add the flour at once, whisking rapidly until the mixture thickens and forms a paste.

3 Reduce to a medium low heat, gradually adding the warm skim milk whisking constantly.

4 The sauce should be thickening. The entire process should take approximately 10 minutes. Salt and pepper to taste.

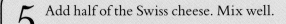

5 Add half of the Swiss cheese. Mix well.

6 Place the cooked cauliflower in a buttered dish. Pour the sauce over the top and sprinkle with the rest of the Swiss cheese and the nutmeg. Bake for 20 minutes or until golden.

Nutrition Information

Serving Size **1 Cup**   Servings **7**

Calories **131**	Potassium . . . . . . **407 mg**
Calories from fat **73**	Total Carbohydrates . . . **12 g**
Total Fat . . . . **8 g**	Dietary Fiber . . . . **2 g**
Cholesterol . . . . . . **24 mg**	Sugars . . . . **5 g**
Sodium . . . . **110 mg**	Protein . . . . **9 g**

Vitamin A . . . . **7 %**	Vitamin B6 . . . . **12 %**
Vitamin C . . . . . . **78 %**	Folic Acid . . . . **15 %**
Calcium . . . . **21 %**	Vitamin B12 . . . . . . **13 %**
Iron . . . . **4 %**	Pantothenic Acid . . . . **9 %**
Vitamin D3 . . . . **3 %**	Phosphorus . . . . **20 %**
Vitamin E . . . . **1 %**	Magnesium . . . . **13 %**
Vitamin K . . . . **20 %**	Zinc . . . . **9 %**
Vitamin B1 . . . . **7 %**	Selenium . . . . **12 %**
Vitamin B2 . . . . **13 %**	Copper . . . . **4 %**
Niacin . . . . **4 %**	Manganese . . . . **19 %**

OTHER BENEFICIAL NUTRIENTS (PER SERVING)

Choline	**56 mg**
Beta-Carotene	**18 mcg**
Lutein & Zeaxanthin	**14 mcg**

BRUSSELS SPROUTS
WITH HAZELNUTS AND THYME

8 SERVINGS • PREPARATION: 10 MINUTES • COOKING: 15 MINUTES • EASY

The most frequent thing I hear about this recipe is, "I really don't like Brussels sprouts, but I love this! This is really different!" It truly is unique and it makes a wonderful, healthy side dish for the holidays, and the hazelnut makes it festive and flavorful. Andrew survived most of his life having never eaten a Brussels sprout, but now, he has become a huge fan, which pleases him no end, since they are among the healthiest of cruciferous vegetables.

2 lbs. Brussels sprouts,
    washed & quartered

1 tbsp. olive oil

1 tsp. balsamic vinegar

⅓ cup chicken broth

¾ cup hazelnuts, finely chopped

1 tsp. agave syrup or honey

1 tsp. butter

Few sprigs of thyme

Salt and freshly ground
    pepper to taste

1 In a large skillet, sauté the Brussels sprouts in olive oil for approximately 5 minutes on high heat until the sprouts develop a golden color. Add the Balsamic vinegar.

2 Add the broth, reduce the heat and simmer for an additional 5 minutes.

3 In a small skillet, brown the hazelnuts for 5 minutes in the agave syrup and butter.

4 Add the hazelnuts to the Brussels sprouts along with the thyme, salt and pepper. Cook for an additional 3 to 5 minutes.

5 Serve hot as a side dish.

Nutrition Information

Serving Size **1 Cup**   Servings **8**

Calories	104	Potassium	254 mg
Calories from fat	80	Total Carbohydrates	3 g
Total Fat	9 g	Dietary Fiber	3 g
Cholesterol	1 mg	Sugars	2 g
Sodium	38 mg	Protein	3 g

Vitamin A	7 %	Folic Acid	10 %
Vitamin C	64 %	Pantothenic Acid	2 %
Calcium	3 %	Phosphorus	6 %
Iron	6 %	Magnesium	7 %
Vitamin E	11 %	Zinc	177 %
Vitamin K	97 %	Selenium	1 %
Vitamin B1	9 %	Copper	11 %
Vitamin B2	3 %	Manganese	41 %
Niacin	3 %		
Vitamin B6	8 %		

OTHER BENEFICIAL NUTRIENTS (PER SERVING)

Omega-3 (ALA+EPA+DPA+DHA)	15 mg
Choline	14 mg
Beta-Carotene	200 mcg
Alpha-Carotene	3 mcg
Lutein & Zeaxanthin	710 mcg

SWEET POTATO SOUFFLÉ WITH PECANS

16 SERVINGS • PREPARATION: 30 MINUTES • COOKING: 50 MINUTES • MEDIUM

Andrew has never loved sweet potatoes – until now. He insists that this could be a dessert and he does not believe the calories can actually be this low. It makes for a lovely classic casserole for the holidays. It truly is like a dessert and the soufflé treatment makes it light, fluffy and low in calories. I use butter here, but you can even eliminate that if you like. I generally serve a ½ cup as a side dish. This adds some delicious variety to any Thanksgiving or holiday meal.

SOUFFLÉ:

4 large sweet potatoes,
   peeled and cubed

2 tbsp. + 1 tsp. butter (optional)

½ cup skim milk

4 egg whites (¾ cup)

¼ cup maple syrup

1 tsp. vanilla extract

TOPPING:

1 cup pecans

½ cup almond meal

¼ cup maple syrup

1 tbsp. butter

1 Preheat oven to 350°. In a steamer basket, steam the sweet potatoes for approximately 15 to 20 minutes until cooked through.

2 Prepare the topping by chopping pecans and mixing them in a small bowl with almond meal and maple syrup. Set aside.

3 Mash the steamed sweet potatoes and 1 tbsp. butter in a large bowl. Stir in skim milk, egg whites, maple syrup and vanilla until smooth. This step can be done in the Cuisinart.

4 Pour the mashed mixture evenly into a buttered baking dish and add the topping along with pats of the remaining butter (optional).

5 Bake for approximately 30 minutes. Serve hot.

Nutrition Information

Serving Size **1/2 Cup**   Servings **16**

Calories	**148**	Potassium	**298 mg**
Calories from fat	**73**	Total Carbohydrates	**20 g**
Total Fat	**8 g**	Dietary Fiber	**2 g**
Cholesterol	**2 mg**	Sugars	**10 g**
Sodium	**26 mg**	Protein	**3 g**

Vitamin A	**2 %**	Folic Acid	**2 %**
Vitamin C	**7 %**	Vitamin B12	**1 %**
Calcium	**3 %**	Pantothenic Acid	**2 %**
Iron	**3 %**	Phosphorus	**6 %**
Vitamin E	**5 %**	Magnesium	**7 %**
Vitamin K	**1 %**	Zinc	**3 %**
Vitamin B1	**6 %**	Selenium	**4 %**
Vitamin B2	**6 %**	Copper	**8 %**
Niacin	**2 %**	Manganese	**25 %**
Vitamin B6	**5 %**		

OTHER BENEFICIAL NUTRIENTS (PER SERVING)

Omega-3 (ALA+EPA+DPA+DHA)	**3 mg**
Choline	**11 mg**
Beta-Carotene	**27 mcg**
Lutein & Zeaxanthin	**1 mcg**

BUTTERNUT SQUASH GRATIN
WITH SAGE AND MACADAMIA NUTS

16 SERVINGS • PREPARATION: 30 MINUTES • COOKING: 60 MINUTES • MEDIUM

I made this dish a couple of years ago for Thanksgiving at our friend Carrie's house and it was a big hit! I set out to make it healthier for this book and amazingly, it turned out even better! Instead of the typical breadcrumbs, I love the Macadamia nut topping. The preparation can be a little time consuming; but it can be made in advance, refrigerated and baked for 45 minutes. Feel free to add more cream to this dish if you wish. I am trying to keep it lower in calories!

6 cups butternut squash,
   peeled & cubed

1 tsp. olive oil

1 large onion, chopped (2 cups)

2 cloves garlic, minced

1 oz. fresh sage, minced

Salt and freshly ground
   pepper to taste

1 tsp. allspice

1 tsp. butter

¼ cup heavy cream

¼ cup skim milk

1 whole egg or 2 egg whites

½ cup Macadamia nuts,
   crushed

1 Preheat oven to 375°. Using a steamer basket, steam the squash for 10 to 15 minutes.

2 Add olive oil to a skillet over medium heat, and sauté the onion and garlic for approximately 8 minutes until golden.

3 Add the steamed squash and sage to the skillet, seasoning with salt, pepper and allspice.

4 Transfer squash mixture to a lightly buttered casserole dish. In a small bowl, whisk together the cream, skim milk and egg. Evenly pour over the gratin mixture.

5 Sprinkle crushed nuts and minced sage on top.

6 Bake for 35 to 40 minutes until bubbly and the nuts are golden. Garnish with sage leaf and serve hot as a side dish.

Nutrition Information

Serving Size **1/2 Cup**   Servings **16**

Calories	**103**	Potassium	**196 mg**
Calories from fat	**66**	Total Carbohydrates	**8 g**
Total Fat	**7 g**	Dietary Fiber	**2 g**
Cholesterol	**6 mg**	Sugars	**2 g**
Sodium	**15 mg**	Protein	**2 g**
Vitamin A	**76 %**	Folic Acid	**4 %**
Vitamin C	**15 %**	Vitamin B12	**1 %**
Calcium	**2 %**	Pantothenic Acid	**2 %**
Iron	**3 %**	Phosphorus	**4 %**
Vitamin E	**4 %**	Magnesium	**6 %**
Vitamin K	**7 %**	Zinc	**2 %**
Vitamin B1	**8 %**	Selenium	**2 %**
Vitamin B2	**3 %**	Copper	**4 %**
Niacin	**3 %**	Manganese	**19 %**
Vitamin B6	**5 %**		

OTHER BENEFICIAL NUTRIENTS (PER SERVING)

Omega-3 (ALA+EPA+DPA+DHA)	**7 mg**
Choline	**3 mg**
Beta-Carotene	**1,491 mcg**
Alpha-Carotene	**292 mcg**
Lutein & Zeaxanthin	**6 mcg**

Muriel and Andrew's Delicious Creamy Corn

16 SERVINGS • PREPARATION: 30 MINUTES • COOKING: 30 MINUTES • MEDIUM

Andrew and I went to a restaurant in Miami where they served the most delicious (and over-the-top decadent) Creamed Corn. We thought it would be nice to include a healthy version in our Holiday Cookbook. I make mine with almost no cream using mostly skim milk. It is a small fraction of the calories of typical Creamed Corn, but everyone just loves it! Removing the corn from the cob can be a messy process, but using a large bowl considerably diminishes the mess! I love fresh corn, but of course, you can also feel free to use frozen sweet corn.

6 ears corn (yields about
   8 cups of kernels)

3 tbsp. butter plus
   1 tsp. for baking dish

1 red onion, chopped

½ tsp. turmeric

1 tbsp. agave syrup or honey

Salt and freshly ground
   pepper to taste

2 tbsp. yellow cornmeal
   (fine or medium grind)

1 tbsp. cornstarch

1½ cups warm skim milk

2 tbsp. heavy cream
   (optional)

1 sprig of rosemary,
   crushed

1 Preheat oven to 350°. In a large bowl, place each ear of corn in a vertical position and use a knife to remove the kernels down to the pulp from top to bottom. Scrape as much of the pulp as possible.

2 In a large skillet over medium heat, melt 1 tbsp. of butter and sauté the onion for about 5 minutes.

3 Add corn, turmeric, agave syrup, salt and pepper. Cook on medium heat for 10-15 minutes, stirring regularly until corn is tender.

4 In a small saucepan over medium heat, make a roux with 2 tbsp. butter, cornmeal and cornstarch, whisking until it makes a paste. Slowly add the skim milk, continuously whisking approximately 5 to 8 minutes until creamy. Whisk in the heavy cream at the very end.

5 Place the corn in a casserole dish or large iron skillet, pour the roux over it and sprinkle with the crushed rosemary.

6 Bake for approximately 15 minutes. Serve hot.

Nutrition Information

Serving Size **1/2 Cup**   Servings **16**

Calories	113	Potassium	238 mg
Calories from fat	23	Total Carbohydrates	19 g
Total Fat	3 g	Dietary Fiber	2 g
Cholesterol	4 mg	Sugars	7 g
Sodium	31 mg	Protein	3 g

Vitamin A	4 %	Folic Acid	2 %
Vitamin C	9 %	Vitamin B12	1 %
Calcium	2 %	Pantothenic Acid	6 %
Iron	3 %	Phosphorus	9 %
Vitamin D	1 %	Magnesium	9 %
Vitamin E	1 %	Zinc	3 %
Vitamin B1	9 %	Selenium	2 %
Vitamin B2	4 %	Copper	2 %
Niacin	7 %	Manganese	7 %
Vitamin B6	4 %		

OTHER BENEFICIAL NUTRIENTS (PER SERVING)

Omega-3 (ALA+EPA+DPA+DHA)	6 mg
Choline	20 mg
Beta-Carotene	39 mcg
Alpha-Carotene	13 mcg
Lutein & Zeaxanthin	493 mcg

PUMPKIN "PIE" PARFAITS

8 SERVINGS • PREPARATION: 20 MINUTES • COOKING: 5 MINUTES • EASY

We all have our favorite family dessert recipes, but I was looking for a new and different spin on Pumpkin Pie. I think Andrew had already had enough of regular pumpkin pie and since we don't eat gluten at our house, I thought it would be fun and simple to make small pumpkin puddings (mini-pies in a cup) using heart-healthy nuts to create the "crust." He absolutely loves these and of course, he reminds me of how nutritious pumpkin is. These can be made a day ahead and refrigerated, but don't make the whipped cream until serving. Delicious and low in calories!

1½ cups heavy whipping cream

2 tsp. powdered sugar

¼ cup pecans and walnuts, crushed

⅓ cup fat-free cream cheese or whipped cream cheese

2 tsp. vanilla

1 15 oz. can pure pumpkin (not pie mix)

1 tsp. pumpkin pie spice

½ tsp. cinnamon

2 tbsp. sweet condensed milk

¼ cup skim milk (more as needed)

1.5 oz. pack/box vanilla fat-free, sugar-free, instant pudding mix

1 In a heavy bowl combine the whipping cream with the sugar and half the vanilla. Beat with an electric mixer, cover with plastic wrap and chill.

2 Toast the pecans and walnuts in a pan for 5 minutes and set aside.

3 In a small bowl whisk together the cream cheese and the remaining vanilla until smooth. Slowly fold in the pumpkin, pumpkin spice, cinnamon and condensed milk. Mix in the skim milk and pudding mix.

4 Layer the pumpkin "pie" mixture and the whipped cream in small glasses. Refrigerate for at least two hours before serving. Garnish with crushed nuts.

Nutrition Information

Serving Size **3/4 Cup**   Servings **8**

Calories	296	Potassium	292 mg
Calories from fat	194	Total Carbohydrates	17 g
Total Fat	22 g	Dietary Fiber	1 g
Cholesterol	66 mg	Sugars	11 g
Sodium	184 mg	Protein	9 g

Vitamin A	190 %	Vitamin B6	4 %
Vitamin C	5 %	Folic Acid	4 %
Calcium	16 %	Vitamin B12	6 %
Iron	6 %	Pantothenic Acid	7 %
Vitamin D	4 %	Phosphorus	19 %
Vitamin E	10 %	Magnesium	10 %
Vitamin K	13 %	Zinc	6 %
Vitamin B1	5 %	Selenium	5 %
Vitamin B2	14 %	Copper	7 %
Niacin	2 %	Manganese	19 %

OTHER BENEFICIAL NUTRIENTS (PER SERVING)

Choline	29 mg
Beta-Carotene	3,948 mcg
Alpha-Carotene	2,702 mcg
Lutein & Zeaxanthin	1 mcg

BLUEBERRY AND PECAN CRUMBLE

8 SERVINGS • PREPARATION: 15 MINUTES • COOKING: 25 – 30 MINUTES • EASY

Our friend Tobey gave me the inspiration for this delicious crumble. She is a wonderful cook and makes the best ultra-high calorie Apple Crumble that any human being has ever tasted. My goal was to achieve as much of that flavor as possible and do so with a fraction of the calories. Andrew says I have succeeded. This recipe can be made with any seasonal fruit, but Andrew specifically requested colorful berries, such as blueberries, blackberries, raspberries or even cherries because of their high concentrations of protective compounds.

6 cups blueberries, blackberries
    or raspberries, washed

1 lemon, juiced

4 tbsp. agave syrup
    (or maple syrup or honey)

¾ cup quick cooking rolled oats

¾ cup almond meal

1 tsp. cinnamon

1 tsp. vanilla extract

¾ cup pecans, crushed

3 tbsp. butter, melted

1 Preheat oven to 375°. In a large bowl mix the berries with lemon juice, 2 tbsp. of the syrup and cinnamon.

2 Prepare the crumble by combining the oats, almond meal, cinnamon, vanilla, remaining agave syrup, crushed pecans and melted butter. Quickly mix with your fingers.

3 Transfer berries into a buttered baking dish.

4 Top berry mixture with crumble.

5 Bake for 25 to 30 minutes. Serve with vanilla ice cream or freshly whipped cream.

Nutrition Information

Serving Size **1 Cup**   Servings **8**

Calories	285	Potassium	229 mg
Calories from fat	156	Total Carbohydrates	27 g
Total Fat	17 g	Dietary Fiber	6 g
Cholesterol	11 mg	Sugars	14 g
Sodium	40 mg	Protein	5 g

Vitamin A	4 %	Vitamin B6	5 %
Vitamin C	22 %	Folic Acid	4 %
Calcium	5 %	Pantothenic Acid	4 %
Iron	7 %	Phosphorus	12 %
Vitamin D	1 %	Magnesium	14 %
Vitamin E	19 %	Zinc	8 %
Vitamin K	28 %	Selenium	4 %
Vitamin B1	11 %	Copper	15 %
Vitamin B2	10 %	Manganese	69 %
Niacin	5 %		

OTHER BENEFICIAL NUTRIENTS (PER SERVING)

Omega-3 (ALA+EPA+DPA+DHA)	90 mg
Choline	20 mg
Beta-Carotene	47 mcg
Lutein & Zeaxanthin	106 mcg

BLACK & WHITE CAKE

15 SERVINGS • PREPARATION: 30 MINUTES • COOKING: 45 MINUTES • DIFFICULT

This is a rich, dark-chocolate, flourless cake combined with our vanilla cheesecake. Everyone who has tried it loves it and can't believe it's so low in calories. Andrew loves it as a source of chocolate's protective compounds, so be sure to use a quality chocolate, high in cocoa solids. We prefer 70% to 85% cocoa solids. I serve it with a small dollop of whipped cream. Believe me, there is nothing "diet-tasting" about this dessert, but you will be surprised at how much we succeeded in reducing its sugar and calorie content. It will be a big hit over the holidays!

CHOCOLATE CAKE:

1 stick of butter (4 oz. plus
   1 tsp. for baking dish)

9 to 10 oz. dark chocolate,
   coarsely chopped, about 3 bars

5 large eggs, separated into yolks
   and whites

⅓ cup granulated sugar

1 tsp. vanilla extract

1 tbsp. espresso (optional)

¼ tsp. cream of tartar

VANILLA CHEESECAKE:

8 oz. "⅓ Less Fat" cream cheese

1 tsp. vanilla extract

2 tbsp. granulated sugar

1 large egg

WHIPPED CREAM:

(optional)

1½ cup heavy
   whipping cream

2 tbsp. granulated sugar

1 tsp. vanilla extract

1 Preheat oven to 325°. Grease a non-stick baking dish with 1 tsp. butter.

2 **CHOCOLATE CAKE:** In a saucepan under LOW HEAT, melt the butter and chocolate. Whisk often and remove from heat once done.

3 In a medium bowl add 5 egg yolks, 1/3 cup sugar and vanilla. Beat with an electric whisk until it forms a pale yellow appearance.

4 Fold in the melted chocolate/butter mixture SLOWLY. Add the espresso (optional).

5 In another bowl, beat the egg whites with the cream of tartar using an electric mixer until soft peaks forms.

6 Slowly mix the chocolate mixture into the egg whites with a spatula. Don't "break" the whites while doing it.

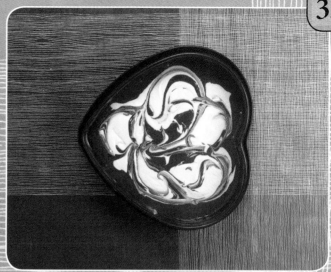

7 **CHEESECAKE:** In a medium bowl mix the cream cheese, vanilla and sugar with an electric mixer until very smooth. Add the egg and beat until there are no lumps left.

8 Pour chocolate mixture into baking dish. Add the cheese cake mixture and slowly cut through back and forth with spatula edge to create marble effect. Do not blend.

9 Bake for 40 to 45 minutes. Let cool before cutting to serve.

10 **WHIPPED CREAM** *(optional)*: Beat COLD heavy whipping cream, sugar and vanilla with an electric mixer until peaks form at the top, approximately 5 minute. Be careful not to blend much longer as the mixture can turn into butter! Serve on the side of your decadent Black & White Cake!

Nutrition Information

Serving Size **1 Slice**   Servings **15**

Calories	**210**	Potassium	**171 mg**
Calories from fat	**147**	Total Carbohydrates	**13 g**
Total Fat	**16g**	Dietary Fiber	**2 g**
Cholesterol	**27 mg**	Sugars	**9 g**
Sodium	**148 mg**	Protein	**3 g**

Vitamin A	**6 %**	Folic Acid	**1 %**
Calcium	**4 %**	Vitamin B12	**4 %**
Iron	**11 %**	Pantothenic Acid	**2 %**
Vitamin D	**2 %**	Phosphorus	**8 %**
Vitamin E	**10 %**	Magnesium	**10 %**
Vitamin K	**2 %**	Zinc	**5 %**
Vitamin B1	**1 %**	Selenium	**3 %**
Vitamin B2	**3 %**	Copper	**15 %**
Niacin	**1 %**	Manganese	**17 %**
Vitamin B6	**1 %**		

OTHER BENEFICIAL NUTRIENTS (PER SERVING)

Choline	**4 mg**
Beta–Carotene	**17 mcg**
Alpha–Carotene	**1 mcg**
Lutein & Zeaxanthin	**5 mcg**

INDEX

NOTES

NOTES